This '

Creating Winning CVs & Applications

Kathleen Houston

TROTMAN

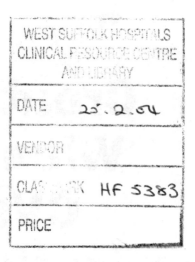
This first edition published in 1998 by Trotman and Company Ltd
12 Hill Rise, Richmond, Surrey TW10 6UA

© Trotman and Company Limited 1998

British Library Cataloguing in Publication Data
A catalogue record for this book is available from the British Library

ISBN 0 85660 303 1

Typeset by Trotman and Company, Richmond
Printed and bound in Great Britain by Creative Print & Design (Wales) Ltd

Contents

Dedication

To my loving and wonderful husband John, without whom which etc
For keeping the hoards or hounds at bay
For Ben who never complained
For Sam who shouted a lot
For Josh who always drives me crazy
For Hannah for keeping me netballing
For Jack who kept wanting to talk to me

About the author

Kathleen Houston is an experienced Careers Adviser working both with young people in schools and colleges and with adult jobseekers. Having experienced the common problems of many career returners after her own rather long career break, she researched effective jobseeking strategies with employers nationally and regionally, with particular reference to CVs and application forms. She discovered that most jobseekers were not doing themselves justice in the application process. Her research worked in a personal way as she gained employment herself, winning not one, but two part-time contracts to suit her personal and family circumstances.

She is committed to helping people improve their chances of success and finds her work fascinating and rewarding. Kathleen has also been involved in CV and jobsearch workshops in her role as an adult guidance worker with a Lancashire college and she writes regularly on jobseeking issues. Most recently she has been an expert on national radio helping the long-term unemployed with advice and support. She is also the author of *Getting into Job Opportunities*, published by Trotman.

CHAPTER 1 First things first

A curriculum vitae (now known universally as a CV) is rarely a thing of beauty, rarely a creative masterpiece, rarely even mildly interesting, and yet this rather dull document has the power to change lives if viewed with the right degree of respect. It deserves respect, because it ought to encapsulate a living, breathing person, but too often it is as dead as its Latin title.

It is easy to misunderstand the purpose of a CV, because there are so many, mystifying, sometimes positively alien forms out there, which can make people think that a CV, a good CV, is a tricky thing to pin down and an even more frustrating thing to create.

Relax! The reality is so humdrum. Replace that picture of a mystifying, nebulous creature with the far more prosaic jelly mould.

On jelly moulds

Consider how the jelly mould forms the shape of the jelly, but never changes the taste, consistency or colour of the jelly. So too, the CV format (the mould) should support and display the real person (the jelly). If this image seems whimsical, stay with it, as it is infinitely preferable to the idea of a CV as a formal, stultifying document that sucks the life out of real people, and leaves at best a bland impression, at worst a dead one.

And so, three basic points have to be explored by anyone wishing to create a true, vibrant, striking CV:

1. The jelly has to be stirred up – the person has to be self-aware enough to know their strengths, abilities, skills, personal characteristics, and decide what is to be displayed in the CV.
2. The mould (the format, shape, layout, the words used) has to be chosen to display the person to best advantage.

3. The person has to decide the purpose of the CV (what it is meant to achieve).

But enough of jelly mould metaphors, let's move on to what you want. You might want a take-away CV, and you might be lucky, as there are enough to choose from in these pages. However, this book is meant to give you the confidence to create an individual, striking CV – one as unique as you. Take the time to look at a variety of CVs, a few bad ones and many good ones, in different styles, layouts and with varied use of language. You may actually need several different CV formats depending on the different jobs that interest you. You really can do this. Just give yourself the chance to develop your own CV style.

Bad, mediocre or just boring CVs made good

Let's take a look at some CVs that are still in the ugly duckling stage, and see them transformed. We can begin with a very traditional, older style CV that still seems to turn up regularly on recruiters' desks.

The metal coathanger CV

Here's what it looks like.

CURRICULUM VITAE

Name: Matthew Pullover
Address: 64 Preston Street, Jumperton, Clotheshire, CL1 2XF
Date of birth: 2 February 1977
Marital status: Single

EDUCATION
Jumperton Secondary School - GCSEs 1993: English A; Geography B; Spanish B; French C; Maths D; History D; Biology E
Jumperton College - 1993-95: BTec National Certificate in Business and Finance

EMPLOYMENT
1993-95 Jumperton Building Society, Clerical Assistant, Main duties - filing, photocopying and typing.
1995-present Clotheshire Building Society, Customer Service Clerk. Main duties - dealing with counter service, processing queries.

INTERESTS Canoeing, basketball, stamp collecting

REFERENCES Available on request.

> Please don't do one like this!

Of course this type of CV is simple and some might say it has a certain minimalist style, but don't count on this unassuming creature to grab (let alone hold) attention. It doesn't work, because it is barely more than a list of qualifications and experience. While it almost says 'Guess what I'm like?' it is not intriguing enough to tempt the reader past the first few lines. It does not entice the eye or suggest a real person desiring real job opportunities. Metal coathangers are not used in designer shops or in window displays, because they barely hold the shape and weight of the clothes, let alone display them to advantage. So don't pick a metal coathanger CV!

However, even this type of CV can be improved, without changing the words, just by a change of format.

The covered metal coathanger (to cover its nakedness!)

CURRICULUM VITAE
Matthew Pullover
64 Preston Street
Jumperton, Clotheshire, CL1 2XF
Tel: 01987 234500

> This is looking better with the block heading and clearer sections, but:
> ■ the title 'Curriculum Vitae' is wasted space – it is obviously a CV
> ■ most people's 'Education' section is boring, so why put it first?

Education

Jumperton Secondary School
GCSEs 1993   English A, Geography B, Spanish B, French C,
                       Maths D, History D, Biology E

Jumperton College
1993–95   BTec National Certificate in Business and Finance

Employment

1993–95   Jumperton Building Society – Clerical Assistant
                    Main duties – filing, photocopying and typing.
1995–present   Clotheshire Building Society
                    Customer Service Clerk
                    Main duties – dealing with counter service, processing queries.

Interests

Canoeing, basketball, stamp collecting

References

Available on request.

As can be seen, format alone and some basic wordprocessing can partly transform a CV, even one with a substance deficit! Beware though – there are plenty of brilliantly designed CVs around which are absolutely meaningless. There are even some that are frankly too wordprocessed, using every available design trick, so they end up looking like an overdecorated Christmas tree.

To improve this CV further we need to deal with the substance, as a CV without it is like a beautifully wrapped present which turns out to be a rather boring pair of socks.

Here is a much improved version of that very basic CV with format, layout, language and substance on show.

Matthew Pullover
64 Preston Street
Jumperton
Clotheshire CL1 2XF
Tel: 01987 234500

An experienced and qualified building society administration assistant with substantial customer service experience, seeking financial planning opportunities.

Key Skills and Achievements

- Business skills, developed and improved through administration experience and achievement of BTec National Certificate through part-time study via accelerated course.
- Communication skills required in present and previous employment, both with customers and colleagues.
- Information technology skills, being familiar with Finan and Windows computer packages.
- Leadership skills, derived from outdoor pursuits and most recently from achievement of Duke of Edinburgh Award.

Employment

1993–95   Jumperton Building Society – Clerical Assistant
               Promoted from basic office junior to clerical assistant, then given responsibility for particular customer accounts.

1995–present   Clotheshire Building Society
               Customer Service Clerk, involving full responsibility for new accounts and marketing new services; particular training undertaken in teamwork and problem solving, with organisation of improved working practices, having increased department revenue by 50%.

Jumperton Secondary School
GCSEs 1993

English	A	Geography	B	Spanish	B
French	C	Maths	D	History	D
Biology	E				

Jumperton College
1993–95   BTec National Certificate in Business and Finance, with specialist modules in marketing, finance and human resource.

In my spare time I enjoy most outdoor pursuits, which have developed my self-confidence and interpersonal skills. I have represented the county in canoeing and was a runner-up in the recent County Finals.
I am sociable, energetic and enthusiastic and have been able to use these characteristics in my employment to date. I am very motivated and would be prepared to train and study further to benefit any future employer and to fulfil my own potential.

Excellent references available on request.

This CV is better because it has the three important 'L's:

- **layout** – clear, well-presented information
- **logical** – the sequence of sections works to the writer's advantage, with more interesting stuff first and last
- **lively** – or alive – there is a sense of a living breathing person behind the words and format.

CHAPTER 3
CV groundrules

It is useful to start with the groundrules for a good CV, based on research with large and small, regional, national and multi-national employers and what they say they want.

Format rules

- Two pages A4 (third page only if absolutely necessary, but try to avoid this).
- Perfectly wordprocessed document in fairly standard font and size (not italic), justified (both margins straight) and well laid out.
- Logical, easy-to-read layout with lots of white space between sections for definition.
- Good quality paper in reasonable weight, in white or perhaps cream for traditional occupations; possibly coloured paper for artistic/creative careers.
- Central block heading with essential personal information and contact details. Avoid putting age, marital status and other non-relevant details.
- Bold or highlighted headings for all sections (see CV skeleton, pages 47–48).

Content and substance rules

- Place a Career Objective (sometimes given the heading 'Profile') or self-marketing statement underneath the central block heading. Essentially this is who you are and what you want.
- Analyse your key skills and achievements (see CV Planner

 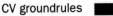

Extraordinaire, pages 48–49) and list them in a block under the Career Objective/Self-Marketing Statement.

- Write an interesting, human 'Personal' section for the end of the CV, which expresses the quintessential 'You'. (Human Resource staff often scan CVs in seconds, by looking at the beginning and then skimming to the end, so finish with a flourish.)
- Use positive, dynamic, concise, precise language.
- Give evidence for skills and abilities wherever possible.
- Juggle sections around within the main body of the CV to emphasise or de-emphasise certain areas. For example, on younger people's CVs the Education section often precedes the Employment section, but for more experienced, less qualified applicants work history might be better placed first to de-emphasise a less impressive education history.
- Decide on chronology or reverse chronology (starting at the present and working backwards date-wise is most usual) for the CV, according to particular needs.

So how does anyone ever create a CV with all this to bear in mind? Well, it's as easy as collecting photos of yourself at different ages and putting them together in an album – the art is the preparation and thought that goes into it.

The idea here is that by looking at a variety of types and styles of CV you will be fired with enthusiasm to create a sparkling, individual CV; but if you're not the fired-up type and want to steal a few ideas here and there then do it that way. Bear in mind the type of job you wish to target as, for example, certain professions may demand a more formal, traditional CV than others – compare the CVs for Bar School with the Media/Advertising ones.

College student CV

Sam Cameron
10 Abbey Walk
Pemberton PT5 5RT
01987 123456

A highly competitive, extrovert, all-round sportsman looking for the chance to use sporting interest, lively reporting style and outgoing personality in a media-related area.

KEY ACHIEVEMENTS AND SKILLS

Leadership skills, having captained college team to British Schools Final resulting in success at winning National Football Colleges Cup.

Sporting skill, both playing and captaining rugby, basketball, cricket and football teams with trials for county rugby and football.

Social skills, used in a variety of settings, in particular in pub hospitality part-time work.

Presentation/performance skills required in drama coursework and in sports captaincy situations, where speeches are often necessary.

Sales skills, evidenced by ability to sell 'unpopular' college poetry magazines at recent Open Evening with success of selling three times as many as other sales 'colleagues'.

EDUCATION

June 1997   GCSEs passed in Maths (B), English Language (A), English Literature (A), Science (AA), Drama (B), History (A), German (C) and Home Economics (C).

Present   Taking three A-levels including Media Studies, Business Studies and History with predicted grades A/B.

WORK EXPERIENCE

Hospitality and catering experience in pub with NVQ passed.
School placement at Red Wing Radio as media assistant.

INTERESTS

I am an active, sporty person who loves meeting people. I am confident in any performance situation and was recently interviewed on radio about my college team's outstanding performance at football.

In a family of three brothers and one sister, we are all football mad and compete to have the best football and sporting knowledge. I can talk and write interestingly about football, but I am also good with people and like to encourage them to talk about their own enthusiams.

Excellent references available on request.

Résumé style CVs

This first CV for Sam Cameron is what is known as a résumé style CV – a one-page document that suits certain people's situations. In many cases a one-page résumé can give a better impression and certainly has more impact than a two-page version that is thin on information. It is worth considering this CV mutation for many reasons, but especially if an applicant wishes to blitz a large number of employers speculatively, as it certainly reduces the cost of stationery and postage.

Let's look at the beginning of a rather long four-page CV, which did not really do the writer justice, and probably bored the reader in the first few lines.

VERONICA BETTS
16 Lowly Avenue
Harton
ZX2 BY4
Tel: 0128 451 1540

Balks Cash and Carry   April 1992 to date
Receptionist
* Switchboard
* Booking in all customers on computer; registering new customers
* Dealing with customer enquiries

This rather relentless, list type CV, continued by detailing the minutiae of every job undertaken over a period of nine years. It was accurate, honest and packed with information, but essentially as interesting as a laundry list.

When someone has by choice enjoyed a variety of employment fields it is difficult to present this on a CV without suggesting lack of dedication or staying power; in addition, a litany of job descriptions makes the CV an endurance test for the reader. Certain employers may demand a more objective, list type CV with limited personal, subjective information and a less marketing style, but even when specifically requested, perhaps within the application information provided by some companies, a certain economy of detail and a concise approach is desirable.

Just as a good hairdresser can look at a person and suggest the best hairstyle for the look and lifestyle of the client, so CV guidance would concentrate on the impression Veronica wants to create and advise a simpler, more punchy, less detailed document with a more individual style.

What worked for Veronica was some rather ruthless cutting to produce a one-page résumé style CV.

Following it you'll find another résumé for a technician engineer, created on the same principles of meticulous pruning, so that only essential information is displayed, resulting in a document with considerable impact.

Résumé style CV version one

VERONICA BETTS
16 Lowly Ave
Harton ZX2 BY4
Tel: 0128 451 1540

A confident, flexible communicator with excellent social skills and varied work experience in retail and business areas, telesales, direct sales and customer service in a wide range of occupations.

Relevant Skills

- Interpersonal and social skills used in all employment and experience to date.
- Communication skills – both verbal and written, particularly used in recent Trade Development managerial role.
- Customer service skills and experience from retail, wholesale and direct sales environments.
- Flexibility and adaptability, proven by ability to juggle two and three part-time work contracts at the same time.
- Business/information technology/keyboard skills – particularly connected with customer databases and computerised mail order systems.

Employment History

June 94 – April 1998   Balks Cash and Carry
Assistant Trade Development Manager
Promotion to this post, which involved visiting customers for promotional purposes, canvassing and registering prospective and new customers over a regional area, analysis of computer reports and public relations work.

August 93 – June 94	*Purchase order clerk* as above Responsible for processing product orders and maintenance of computer systems including telesales on a day-to-day basis.
April 92 – August 93	*Receptionist* as above Duties included dealing with customer enquiries and registration, financial transactions and general admin.
June 91 – April 92	*Beauty Product Sales Consultant* Full customer service offered, responding to deadlines and sales targets.
May 89 – June 91	*Customer Service Clerk* for a mail order company General mail order service and telesales, including problem solving, returns and clerical duties
Dec 86 – May 89	Various part-time jobs undertaken, many in parallel, including work for the Royal Mail, business stocktaking and department store demonstrations.

Education

This took place at Blessed Margaret School, Balton. I have a good fluency in spoken French.

Recently I completed a short course on interior decorative techniques at Harton College.

Personal

I have undertaken a variety of jobs which have helped me to be multi-skilled and adaptable. These have included calculating bets for a local bookmaker, working for an accountant and catering at various levels. In my spare time I enjoy music, sewing and cookery.

This résumé is now a far more concise version of Veronica's life than the original, and manages to convey the wealth of experience she was able to offer in a more effective way. The self-marketing statement at the beginning is deliberately unspecific, as she wanted to use this résumé to stimulate a range of different types of jobs with different employers.

Résumé style CVs are also very useful for speculative applications as they are a snapshot view of the applicant, which can often be highly effective in catching an employer's attention. Recruiters' time is limited and it has been proven that if unsolicited CVs are read at all (some employers refuse to accept them), the concise, attractive and unique ones are most likely to be considered favourably. It can be difficult to cram a full life into one page, but it is worth the effort, because when done well it has real impact. Remember how a small piece of chocolate can taste better than a whole bar, how the taste lingers in your mouth, tempting you to ask for more. Similarly an employer must be enticed to consider an applicant and a good résumé will do this. A fuller CV can be forwarded on request or taken to an interview.

It's worth noting that a full two-page CV can be the basis for a résumé with a bit of ruthless cutting and some companies, particularly American ones, demand a one-page résumé, as a way of testing your ability to summarise and present facts succinctly. On the subject of American companies, it is also fairly common to have photos of the applicant on CVs; so if you are applying to multinational American organisations, consider whether to follow this custom. It might be advisable for those occupations where personal presentation is considered important (the media, major airlines and customer-focused areas), but should be used with care, and only by those who are reasonably photogenic!

A final point on American customs – 'résumé' is the usual American term for a CV and can be one or two pages. Without making impertinent generalisations, it does appear that American résumés are more flamboyant than European ones; a typical unassuming English CV might only be read by American recruiters for its novelty value.

So again it appears that anyone writing a CV/résumé must match it to the job, company or profession to create a CV that works – ie gets you an interview!

Next you'll find another résumé version, followed by the fuller CV for the same person, so the ruthless editing can be admired.

Résumé style CV version two (Technician Engineer)

Gary Stephens
10 Tremon Close, West Harrington
Liverpool L99 5RD
0151 39871

A fully qualified technician engineer with experience of electrical/electronic work, seeking employment in quality control engineering or related engineering functions.

Relevant skills
Communication skills used in inspecting/testing and in quality control with the ability to communicate quality issues to colleagues
Teamwork skills necessary in various technical projects
Quality control skills to oversee/monitor and maintain quality of output
Information technology skills appropriate to technical work area

Employment History
I am presently employed in the switchgear quality control department at a voltage equipment company as a quality engineer working to ISO standards. My duties are to ensure the quality standards of the air circuit breaker section, using a 100% checking system. In addition, I am called upon to inspect the feeder shops, ie machine shop, paint shop and goods inward, as required.

Training and Experience: 1993–1997
I have completed a 4-year apprenticeship with ADC Equipment as an electrical engineer. Basic training included one year at Harrington College covering subjects such as wiring to IEL regulations, basic electronics, basic fitting, machining and fabrication work.

Three years' training at ADC followed which consisted of work in the following departments. Assembly line: assembling and wiring system switchboards, circuit breakers, fuse switches. Test inspection: performing electrical test and inspection of air circuit breakers, current transformers and switchboards. Quality control: monitoring the quality of the products in the switchgear department.

Education and Qualifications
1984–89	St Peter's School, Harrington
	8 GCSEs achieved with Maths (C), English (C), Engineering Practice (C) and Geometrical Drawing (B).
1989–93	Harrington College
	City and Guilds Electronics and Electrical Craft Studies – Part 1. Units towards Part 2 completed.
1997	Harrington College
	BTec National Certificate achieved while working, through part-time study.

Personal Interests
In my spare time I enjoy sporting activities, mainly five-a-side football. I also enjoy playing chess and have a keen interest in animals.

Technician Engineer CV

Gary Stephens
10 Tremon Close, West Harrington
Liverpool L99 5RD
0151 39871

A fully qualified technician engineer with experience of electrical/electronic work, seeking employment in quality control engineering or related engineering functions.

Relevant skills
Communication skills used in inspecting/testing and in quality control with the ability to communicate quality issues to colleagues
Teamwork skills necessary in various technical projects
Quality control skills to oversee/monitor and maintain quality of output
Information technology skills appropriate to technical work area

Employment History

Present working situation
I am currently employed in the switchgear quality control department at a voltage equipment company as a quality engineer working to ISO standards. My duties are to ensure the quality standards of the air circuit breaker section, using a 100% checking system. In addition, I am also called upon to inspect the feeder shops, ie, machine shop, paint shop and goods inward, as required.

Training and Experience

1993–1997 I have completed a 4-year apprenticeship with ADC Equipment as an electrical engineer.
Basic training included one year at Harrington College covering subjects such as wiring to IEL regulations, basic electronics, basic fitting, machining and fabrication work.
I then had three years' training at ADC, which consisted of work in the following departments:
- Assembly line: assembling and wiring system switchboards, circuit breakers, fuse switches.
- Test inspection: performing electrical test and inspection of air circuit breakers, current transformers and switchboards.
- Quality control: monitoring the quality of the products in the switchgear department.

April 96 Selected for Internal Quality Audit Training Course.

Nov 96 Modular training programme undertaken, pertaining to the operation and maintenance of finishing equipment.

Feb 97 Training in analysis methods for Pyroclean 205.

June 97 Passed electrical conversion course.

July 97 Completed Electricity at Work Regulations.

Education and Qualifications

1984–89   St Peter's School, Harrington
             8 GCSEs achieved with Maths (C), English (C), Engineering Practice (C) and Geometrical Drawing (B).
1989–93   Harrington College
             City and Guilds Electronics and Electrical Craft Studies – Part 1. Units towards Part 2 completed.
1997   Harrington College
             BTec National Certificate achieved while working, through part-time study.

Personal Interests

In my spare time I enjoy sporting activities, mainly five-a-side football. I also enjoy playing chess and have a keen interest in animals.

Referees
[Names and addresses of referees]

This CV had to promote the skills of someone trained to technical level in engineering. Enough detail is displayed to show technical expertise but the additional training and courses show motivation and commitment, so these are included too. The format makes it easy for the reader to find relevant information and the shaded block at the beginning emphasises key skills on offer.

Administrative Assistant CV

SHIRLEY SAMSON
28 Old Hall Road
Denton Bridge DR2 ER2
0140 98765

An experienced, conscientious administrative assistant, seeking general clerical work, possibly with a caring/charitable organisation.

KEY SKILLS

- Administrative skills over a broad range of clerical work, including complex financial transactions.
- Advanced level information technology skills, having used databases and wordprocessing packages, most recently updated through achievement of qualifications.
- Interpersonal skills from customer service environment of previous employment.
- Flexibility and adaptability from having worked in a large company and in various departments and teams.

- Ability to work under pressure and in challenging situations, most recently in customer complaints section of large organisation.

EMPLOYMENT HISTORY

1990–1997   Central Denshire Corporation
Typist/Clerk/Receptionist
Ensuring the smooth running of the Customer Complaints Section and dealing face to face with often irate customers, required good organisational ability and tact, patience and calmness under pressure.

1986–1990   Atticus Handcrafts
Personal Assistant to Sales Office Manager
Responsible for checking orders, and making out invoices/credit transactions.

1983–1986   Shatron Mechanics
Typist/Receptionist/Switchboard Operator promoted to **PA to Managing Director.**

EDUCATION AND QUALIFICATIONS

1997   Denton Business College
Excel 5 and Word 6 undertaken and passed in 12 weeks

1990–1997   Various in-service courses completed and passed through company training, including **Basic Bookkeeping, Wordprocessing, Angoss/ Smartware, Lotus 1-2-3 Intermediate.**

VOLUNTARY WORK

1983 to present Fundraising undertaken on a regular basis for three local charities, supporting children (local Hospice, Handicapped Children's Holiday Trust and NSPCC).

PERSONAL

I am punctual and reliable and can work individually or as part of a team. I speak confidently with the general public or the business community. I like learning new skills and caring for people, particularly children, and would like the chance to use this side of my personality in my future employment.

In my spare time I enjoy gardening, reading and spending time with my family.

REFERENCES

Excellent references are available on request.

This is a slightly different format with
- all headings centrally blocked,
- key skills, experience and recent training and qualifications emphasised

to show an experienced person with a broad range of skills, still keen to learn more, and to use these skills in the voluntary/charity sector, which her personal interests back up.

This lady was struggling to gain interviews on the basis of her old CV. We wanted to give more emphasis to her experience and skills, rather than her original education, which she had placed as the first section on the CV. As this education just stated that she attended secondary school and gained no qualifications it was a rather negative beginning!

By rearranging the information and deleting the poor education start, we have given a more positive edge to the CV and de-emphasised irrelevant details like her distant education history. This is not untruthful, it is simply leaving out information that has no relevance to her present job search, and making it easy for an employer to see the key aspects of this applicant without being distracted by unnecessary detail. The covering letter she sent with her CV went something like this:

Dear Mr Brown

As you can see from my CV, I possess the administrative and organisational skills to promote your charity to the public, coupled with the breadth of experience and flexibility to deal with any situations that present themselves.

My experience as a voluntary fundraiser for other charities has helped me understand the practical aspects of charity work. I would love to work for your group and be able to support the work with children that you are committed to. I also make a good cup of coffee!

I look forward to meeting you.

Yours sincerely

Shirley Samson

Shirley got the job, but she gained an interview on the basis of the 'good cup of coffee' phrase. She was precisely what the charity wanted – someone with proven skills and experience but with her feet on the ground, so she wasn't above making a cup of coffee.

A very good example of a Personal Assistant CV

SUSAN COTTON
2 Winkle Crescent
Mussels
Berks RG10 2BX
Tel: 01781 773241

A highly experienced secretary/personal assistant with additional expertise in human resource, office management and general educational administration.

Key Skills and Achievements

- Supervisory and management experience through recent human resource recruitment role.
- Excellent communication skills, both verbal and written, in support work to school governors, through experience at Industrial Tribunal and in day-to-day correspondence and contact with teachers and pupils.
- High level secretarial skills developed through broad experience in administration.
- Ability to work under pressure and to deadlines.
- Problem solving skills, used in a various job contracts, whether in administration, hospitality or care experience settings, to assess situations clearly and make prompt, accountable decisions.

Employment History

April 91 to date Cherrington College
Office Manager and Personal Assistant to the Principal
Supervision and management of office and five staff to provide effective and efficient operation of all aspects of college administration, including external and internal correspondence, pupil records and database, personnel duties involving recruitment, shortlisting and interviewing, and secretarial services to the Principal and the governors.

Two jobs at once – what energy!

Nov 92 to date Additional parallel contract working part time as a residential social worker with Adults with Learning Disabilities.

Nov 86–July 91 Self-employed Publican and Restaurateur
With no previous experience of commercial catering I designed the catering kitchen and restaurant, developing the business into a thriving concern, while studying at catering college and gaining City and Guilds Catering qualifications with a Distinction.
Managing the restaurant developed my business skills and proved that I could cope with anything. Customer service required confidence and authority, both of which I possess.

1984–86 Bennelson and Partners, London
Secretary to Partnership, promoted to Personal Assistant to Senior Partner and Chairman.

CV groundrules ■ [:]

| 1982–84 | The Landmark Trust |
| | Junior Secretary |

Education

1988–89	City of Bath College of Further Education
1971–72	Pitmans Secretarial College
	Merit Passes in Shorthand, Typing, Audio Typing, Secretarial Duties, 120wpm shorthand.
	City and Guilds 706/1 Distinction
1966–71	St William's Convent, Radley
	O-level/CSE passes in Maths, English, History, French.

Wonderful character and self-knowledge shown here

Personal

I am a professional, innovative and committed personal assistant with a wide range of experience in administration, management and personnel functions. My experience of other career areas through self-employment and my part-time job has developed my flexibility and adaptability and is proof of my energy and individuality.

I am able to take decisions and act with authority and autonomy if necessary. I communicate effectively to make and build contacts with colleagues and external personnel. I have a good memory and the ability to respond to change. If I were to describe myself, I would say I was calm, confident and diligent.

References

Available on request.

This is an excellent CV with a professional format and plenty of substance. The writer shows she is articulate and self-confident, a really winning combination; and there is an abundance of evidence of skills and experience, despite some rather humble qualifications. This is a person who has stretched herself and responded to challenges in her life in a very successful manner and this is beautifully illustrated in a two-page CV.

Advertising CV

You might not like the advertising CV shown opposite, but it is different and aimed at a pushy industry. It might be different enough to work. Be brave enough to try your own style if you're going for a highly competitive industry.

HANNAH CLAYTON
8 Joshua Street   Boatridge BR2 CR2
01973 349 6455

WHAT YOU NEED TO KNOW ABOUT ME

- ❏ I can write, think, come up with ideas and sell those ideas as advertising concepts.
- ❏ I have boundless energy and enthusiasm. I can make words work to advantage.
- ❏ I can persuade, negotiate and compete.
- ❏ I thrive on challenge. You need me.

WHY YOU REALLY NEED ME

I have the academic background (BA Hons Advertising), the agency experience (sandwich year of course) and the personality and communication skills to make great adverts for you and your clients.

I'm not like your other applicants, because I want to work for you more and I've wanted this for a longer time than all those others. I remember those first rule-breaking ads of yours. (Who else would not mention the name of the product, but expect the buying public to know it!)

Perhaps I'm just selling you a line – perhaps I'm just a product of my own imagination! Well I can prove all this, so just give me the chance to meet you. And anyway, don't you want someone with imagination, a different perspective, an individual line, but someone grounded enough to respect the people out there who buy things, and to be on their level?

BASIC BORING STUFF YOU MIGHT WANT TO KNOW

- ❏ School/College Magazine Editor every year for five years
- ❏ 10 GCSEs (all A*), 5 A-levels (A/B grades) – so I'm an over-achiever, who cares?
- ❏ Sandwich year of university course spent at two agencies (one in Manchester, one in USA – embarrassingly good references and both offered me jobs, but I want to work in London for someone like you!)

ANYTHING ELSE?

Am I too much of a maverick to fit in? No! I love working with other bright minds and bouncing ideas around. I love all that team stuff.

Am I arrogant? Honestly, I can be really humble and quiet when required, and if I sound full of myself it's just that I'm only telling you my good points. You don't need to know anything else.

Give me a work trial or a trial project, if you have any doubts, or check my references!

References
[Names and addresses of impressive references here]

Legal CVs

The legal profession, by nature more formal and traditional, requires CVs to be appropriate to these characteristics. Competition for jobs or training contracts or pupillages is extremely intense with only a very small percentage being successful, so the CV has to showcase ability, skills and experience in a dynamic way, while also being a perfect example of superbly honed communication skills and articulacy. Recruiters in this occupation will be wary of bold, flashy statements unsupported by evidence (evidence being key in the legal business) so this kind of CV has to be the Rolls Royce of CVs – a beautiful classy exterior with a sophisticated purring engine underneath.

As a model for any kind of CV it's a pretty good example to follow in any case, so let's start by looking at a typical one that needs to be super-charged to make it work. This CV has an impressive content which is virtually obscured by its nondescript format.

CURRICULUM VITAE

SUSAN BAMFORD   DoB: 7 March 1961
17 Mackeson Road
Bowton, London SW23 9BJ   Telephone: 0181 666 4322

EDUCATION AND QUALIFICATIONS
1996–97   Inns of Court School of Law Vocational Course
             Harmsworth Entrance Exhibition, Middle Temple
             Results to date: Civil Litigation and Evidence 90%
                               Criminal Litigation and Evidence 86%
1993–96   University of London
             LLB (Hons) First Class
             Winner of the Manton Book Prize – awarded in the final year to the
             best LLB student
             (Degree undertaken while in part-time employment)

This was the first section of the original CV and, as can be seen, it contains some rather impressive information about the applicant. Nonetheless, it was completely failing the writer, because the format was so bland and boring. It was printed out on thin, plain white paper and shouted 'I'm quite clever but unassuming' which for Bar School training might be considered inappropriate. Modesty is invariably the downfall of CV writers, who assume that emphasising good points is somehow dishonest. This applicant was in fact a very impressive candidate, and her lack of self-belief or modesty was a serious mistake.

Let's see how this type of CV could become a winner.

Legal CV version one

Susan Bamford
17 Mackeson Road
Bowton
London SW23 9BJ
0181 666 4322

Key Achievements and Skills

- First Class Honours Degree LLB
- Best final year LLB student – winner of Manton Book Award
- Harmsworth Entrance Exhibition – Middle Temple
- Inns of Law School of Law – results to date:
    Civil Litigation and Evidence 90%
    Criminal Litigation and Evidence 86%
- Communication skills involving public speaking, debating and advocacy
- Interviewing skills derived from previous employment in social services context, more recently honed as a volunteer at Hammersmith Law Centre

Legal Experience

1995	Mini-pupillage
	Chambers of David Bentley
	Criminal Law
1997	Voluntary legal advisor – Hammersmith Law Centre
July 1997	Free Representation Unit Social Security Training

Career History

1993 – present	Locum Project Worker (undertaken in parallel to full-time degree and postgraduate study) for various voluntary/charitable organisations working with young homeless and mentally ill people.
	Counselling, advising and oral representation form a key part of this work.
1989–1993	Residential social worker promoted to Assistant Unit Manager at residential centre for young offenders.
1980–89	Various employment, including agency social work for drug projects and charities for the homeless.

1996–1997	Inns of Court School of Law Vocational Course
1993–1996	University of London – LLB 1st Class Honours
1991–1992	Barton University – BTec Certificate in Management Studies achieved through distance learning
1973–1979	2 A-levels, 5 O-levels.

Personal

I am a highly motivated, energetic individual with good interpersonal skills. I thrive on intellectual challenge and I am achievement oriented as evidenced by my recent qualifications and results.

In my spare time I have varied interests, including reading, horse-racing, music, theatre and politics.

References

[Excellent references were detailed here.]

This is quite a formal CV and is full of concise information which emphasises skills, abilities and achievements. Words are used very effectively, for example phrases like:

> *'Voluntary legal advisor…'*
> *'undertaken in parallel to full-time degree and postgraduate study…'*
> *'promoted to…'*
> *'thrive on intellectual challenge…'.*

These are not vain boasts, but can be backed up with hard evidence, contained in the CV.

The next CV is another version of a legal CV to show how the format can influence the look of the document so effectively. This CV successfully gained the applicant interviews for Bar School pupil-lages, and as she was not by qualification a top-class candidate it was obviously the additional personal information, skills and experience that persuaded employers to consider her.

This applicant printed her CV out as a one-page, double-sided document on cream medium weight paper, which although unusual worked well. More importantly, the simple direct wording conveys a real sense of the person behind the document and brings the CV alive.

Legal CV version two

This concise, logical CV shows the self-awareness of the writer and highlights key relevant work experience for her future career in law.

LUCY FORD
'Cliffbriar'
5 Sussex Gardens, Cherrington
East Sussex SR5 TY7
0160 891765
Student Member of the Honorary Society of Middle Temple

EDUCATION AND QUALIFICATIONS

1996–1997	Inns of Court School of Law Vocational Course (Unconditional Offer) Harrington Scholarship and Blackwell Entrance Exhibition, Middle Temple
1991–1996	Hampton University BA Hons (part time) in Law with Sociology Degree classification 2.1
1989–1990	North East Sussex College of Technology Management and Care Training Course for Proprietors and Managers of Private and Voluntary Care Homes
1986–1996	Various in-service training courses, including: Dealing with Violence at Work; Anti-Discriminatory Practice; Advocacy; HIV/AIDS Training and Working with Groups
1978-1981	Umberto Convent, Wimpton O-levels: Maths C, English Language B, English Literature C, Spoken English B, History B, French B, Religion B, Food and Nutrition B

RELEVANT/LEGAL EXPERIENCE

June 1996	Free Representation Unit Social Security/CICB Training
May 95–present	Member of the Professional Network for the Hampton Advocacy Group
October 1993	Mini-pupillage (particular emphasis on criminal work) Chambers of David Brennan, 33 Bandon Row, London EC4 7CF

EMPLOYMENT HISTORY

1991–present	Royal Borough of Hampton Residential Social Worker in housing project for Adults with a Learning Disability
1986–1991	London Borough of Sunton Residential Social Worker in home for the elderly mentally infirm

Voluntary responsibilities undertaken show motivation and vital advocacy/negotiating skills

POSITIONS OF RESPONSIBILITY

1995–present	Citizen Advocate for Adults with a Learning Disability
1994–1996	Foundation School Governor of local primary school with special responsibility as Chair of Governors' Disciplinary Committee

| 1992–1992 | Field Representative for Combined Studies Law Department, Hampton University |

RELEVANT SKILLS

- I am fluent in Makaton, a simplified sign language derived from British Sign Language for people with communication problems including learning disability, autism, stroke survivors and the deaf and non-speaking community. I am also qualified to teach Makaton.
- I am computer literate and familiar with all Windows wordprocessing packages and with the desktop publishing package PagePlus 3.0.
- I have a clean driving licence and I own a car.

> Excellent communication skills evidenced by articulate CV language, proven oral advocacy skills and exceptional additional sign language ability.

PERSONAL

I have worked in people-centred jobs for ten years and I have good communication skills. I am able to work under pressure despite conflicting demands while remaining positive, flexible and organised. I have completed my part-time degree in five years instead of six and have done shift work including night duties throughout.

In my spare time I am co-leader of a weekly drama group for which I also fundraise and do the desktop publishing. My love of music means I attend concerts whenever possible; I also play the guitar and cello.

REFEREES

| Mary Hopwood | Jane Mells – Manager |
| School of Law, Hampton University | Woodville Community Housing Project |

Fitness Instructor/Gym Manager

Having seen rather an intellectual CV, let's take a look at a very different one for a fitness trainer. The emphasis here is on a mixture of physical and mental suitability for a job, as these attributes are of prime importance. While we might not judge a bank manager so severely if he or she were not a perfect physical specimen, we would undoubtedly be deterred from seeking advice from a fitness trainer who looked less than physically fit. In consequence, this CV has to draw attention not only to the interpersonal and sales type skills of the applicant, but also to his credibility as a fitness adviser who must be seen to be benefiting from his own advice. A photograph showing an attractive and extremely fit young man is entirely appropriate in this case.

Daniel Surrey
121 Dixon Lane
Anthill A13 4XT
01909 552655

> A flattering photo was here – he was a highly athletic man, and the photo more than showed this!

Personal Profile
A confident, outgoing, extrovert fitness consultant with some sales experience seeking a new career direction in the fashion and retail industry, possibly sports/fitness equipment sales.

Key Skills
- Excellent communication skills used in one-to-one consultancy work and through telesales experience
- Organisation and time management skills needed as gym manager
- Persuasive sales and negotiating skills, used for present employment in a customer-driven environment
- High record of achievement fulfilling and exceeding company goals
- Decision-making skills from managerial work with ability to work under pressure and to professional standards, especially in GP referral work, where recommendation and recognition by medical profession is vital.

Career History Résumé

1997 – present	Fitness Consultant/Gym Manager Bolton Leisure Services, Bolton	Two jobs at once is very impressive
1996 – present	GP Referral Officer Sports Development Leisure Services Both contracts undertaken in parallel	
1995–92	Fitness Instructor/Lifeguard Bolton Metro Leisure Services	
1992–91	Professional Footballer Hull City Football Club	No further details needed here as being signed up by two professional clubs speaks for itself!
1991–89	Professional Footballer Bury Football Club	

Education and Training

1992–89	Prestwich College City and Guilds Leisure and Recreation Studies City and Guilds Leisure Management RSA Computer Studies
1988	Aspull High School 5 GCSEs A–C in Maths, English Language and Literature, Business Information Studies, D in Art and CDT
1996–92	Training Qualifications Focus 1 (Instructors) Focus 2 (Advanced Instructors) Circuit Training Coach Nutrition Management GP Referral and GP Counselling Sales and Marketing FA Coaching

Personal

I have been a fitness instructor for three years and have been trained to the highest level, having been Gym Manager for the past year. I am confident and outgoing with a determination to further my career by using my skills and abilities. I believe I have a lot to offer an employer, as I have the enthusiasm and the motivation to give 100% along with proven skills and qualifications.

References

Available on request.

> No false modesty here – what he has to offer is clearly highlighted!

Creative/Artistic Graduate CV

The next is another example of how using a picture can help show the personality behind the CV. This was a delightfully unique CV from a young graduate with an unusual mix of fine art and business skills. It was printed on paper handmade by the writer, and included a characterful self-portrait. A very beautiful hand-drawn picture of Sarah, colour washed in subtle water colours, was next to her address – a unique beginning, showing individuality, creative skills and attention to detail. This was in fact the first page of the CV, with a second page filled with more regular information and standard headings.

Note how Sarah backs up the points she makes by giving proof of how she has developed her skills and abilities.

For the design companies to which Sarah was applying, her combination of creativity and business skills are well emphasised, while her highly personalised CV was perfect evidence of her individuality.

She also used this CV in a unique way, when she called in 'on spec' to design studios and left it as a calling card. She then followed this up with a phone call asking for an appointment to discuss any job opportunities within these studios. Her positive assumption that they would want to see her and her portfolio of brilliant work meant a large number of invitations to interview, resulting in a spate of job offers.

CURRICULUM VITAE

Sarah Hallam
5 Bentley Lane
Benton
BR21 2JN
01818 345679

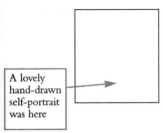

A lovely
hand-drawn
self-portrait
was here

SKILLS

* Communication (interpersonal, written and telephone skills);
  business communication developed through work experience
  involving customer service

* Planning and organising; involved in arranging training and
  development activities for staff in previous short-term employment

* Information technology skills; several years' experience in business
  and academic environments, including wordprocessing,
  spreadsheets, desktop publishing, statistical and graphics packages

* Teamwork; experience of working as part of a team aiming to
  achieve common objectives

* Creative/artistic/design ability, most recently used in design brief for
  multinational advertising company

* Basic French and Spanish conversational ability (two summer
  vacations spent working in Europe).

ACHIEVEMENTS

* Academic success culminating in BA Honours Fine Art with
  Business (Minor module)

* Elected Chairperson of Newnham University Business Link;
  responsible for communication with business and arts organisations
  to promote the work of students

* Completed 'Management Skills' course; four-day residential
  management skills training

Graduate Teacher CV

This graduate teacher CV displays effectively the vital points of a winning CV, with its traditional ordered format but brilliantly customised content. The heart of a living, breathing person beats behind this CV, which is easy on the eye, logical and positive.

Vanessa Connolly
18 Crookings Avenue
Bradley, Cumbria CR5 6FG
01987 765438

> A very clear, well-worded, focused self-marketing statement

A confident, enthusiastic, newly qualified teaching graduate with experience of teaching young people from voluntary work and teaching placements, seeking first-post employment in the mainstream schools sector.

Education and Qualifications

1983–88	Casterton High
	GCSE Maths (C), English (A), English Literature (B), Art and Design (A), History (B), French (B), Biology (B), Chemistry (C).
1988–90	Bradley College
	A-level Art and Design (C), English (B), French (C)
1990–93	Hampton University
	Degree BA (Hons) Art with English 2:1
1994	Operation Raleigh Scheme Award
1994–95	De Graf University
	PGCE Art & Design Education (Pass)

> This kind of experience always impresses, with its combination of service to the community and challenges undertaken within a team situation

Teaching Experience

Sept 94	Saddle Primary School, Saddle Street, Bradley
	Working as Mural Artist on Project with demotivated children.
Oct–Dec 94	New Common College
	Worked as Student Teacher with Year 9
Jan–March 95	Franklin College
	This was my main school-based teaching practice, teaching art, ceramics and textiles to 11–16 year olds.
Easter 95	Research Project Volunteer working with young art students and visually impaired students.

Other Work Experience

1988–90	Hadleys Ltd
	Saturday Waitress
July 93	Playscheme Leader
	Organising summer craft activities for children.
April 94	Volunteer literacy teacher in the community.
Aug 95–present	Temporary work with a major building society.

Relevant Skills
- Artistic skills: mosaic, ceramics, graphics, textiles
- IT skills: familiar with graphics, desktop publishing and word-processing packages
- Interpersonal skills developed through work experience, which has been wholly people focused.

Achievements and Responsibilities
Gymnastic Awards BAGA
Duke of Edinburgh Bronze Award
Netball Captain and House Captain at school.

Personal
I am an outgoing, positive person with leadership and teamwork abilities and an enthusiasm for work with young people. Through Operation Raleigh I had the chance to deal with challenges and discover my own potential, by working with able-bodied and disabled young people on an ethnic arts project, and this developed my awareness of the multi-potentiality of all people, and taught me ways to bring this out.

In my spare time I enjoy visiting art galleries. In addition, I have a keen interest in cinema, music and socialising.

References
Professor Malcolm Kent   Mrs Mary Murphy
[address]   *[address]*

Graduate level Business Manager CV

Anthony O'Neill
32 Minnerton Road
Brunton B34 6ER
01433 654239

―――――――――――――――――――― Profile ――――――――――――――――――――

A successful general manager educated to postgraduate level currently working for a highly successful blue-chip company, being responsible for all aspects of a large 24-hour operation.

A conscientious, motivated individual with proven communication skills who relishes challenges and working under pressure.

―――――――――――――――――― Key Achievements ――――――――――――――――――

- Substantial management experience with responsibility for 400 employees.
- Successfully negotiated and currently managing a £6.5 million budget, including monthly forecasts and reviews.
- Member of senior management team with responsibility for training.
- Credited with successful implementation of company restructuring within target deadlines.

―――――――――――――――――― Career Progression ――――――――――――――――――

April 1995–present   **General Manager**, *Alpha Express*

- Management of all on-site training and Health & Safety requirements for all employees.
- Amicable working relationships with local trade unions developed to achieve swift and successful outcomes on industrial relations matters.
- Management of working practices including disciplinary action where necessary.
- Designated management team member for full day-to-day operational control.
- Introduced staff appraisal scheme/job evaluation to define responsibilities and improve motivation with resulting decline in absenteeism.
- Established and enhanced customer relations by liaison and developing partnerships.

Nov 1995–Mar 1996   **Acting General Manager,** Alpha Express

Oct 1994–Oct 1995   **Management Trainee**, Alpha Express

Sep 1993–Sep 1994   **Business Studies Lecturer,** Neville Chamber College

- Pastoral tutor to 50 students, dealing with student welfare.
- Lecturer on a variety of courses to various academic levels, and to ages 16–65.

Mar 1991–Sep 1991 Business Information Analysis placement at Munificent Bank.

Feb 1990–Sep 1990 Trainee Manager placement at Brunton Health Authority.

1992–1993	Hampton University, PGCE in Business Studies.
1988–1992	Hampton University, BA (Hons) in Business 2(1).
1981–1988	Saint Edward High School A-levels in Economics, Politics 8 GCSEs including Maths and English

——————————————— **Training** ————————————

1996	IPD Certificate in Training.
1997	Supervisory Management Diploma achieved.

Company training undertaken in teambuilding, human resource and customer service.

——————————————— **Personal** ————————————

In my spare time I enjoy martial arts and have achieved Black Belt level. I also keep fit through circuit training and rockclimbing.

I am a motivated, positive, enterprising person and use these characteristics both in my work situation and in my spare time where I act as a business adviser to a local charity.

——————————————— **References** ————————————

Mr Alan Flower
Munificent Bank
Delaware Place
Gainsley
GU3 1HG

Professor Bernard Holly
University of Hampton
Hampton
West Sussex
SU3 HT7

A serious CV for a business graduate who has developed his career through promotion in the same firm. It works because it gives evidence of specific achievements in his management role, such as responsibility for 400 employees, managing a £6.5 million budget and decline in absenteeism brought about by his motivational practices.

ANDREW FRASER
3 GRANTCHESTER ROAD
HASTON, H12 8RT
01200 987652

A committed, experienced marine engineer with varied experience and expertise, seeking career progression into research and development in a large company/organisation.

RELEVANT SKILLS

- Organisational skills, required most recently in second officer role, with responsibility for engine-room maintenance schedules and liaison with shoreside contractors
- Ability to work on own initiative and as part of a team, vital to the smooth running of onboard operations
- Effective communication skills, particularly useful in generating cooperation for immediate action/response
- Ability to exercise quick decisions, remaining calm in emergency situations or while working under extreme pressure
- Training and supervisory skills, used most recently as Cadet Training Officer for engineering department.

CAREER HISTORY AND PROFESSIONAL QUALIFICATIONS

ROYAL FLEET AUXILIARY

1983–87   Marine Engineering Cadet, achieving Phase 1 to 3 of City and Guilds Professional Certificate, covering technician marine engineering practice, electrotechnology and applied mechanics; sea service practical training assessed by Merchant Navy Training Board culminating in Advanced Certificate.

1987–89   4th Officer (Engineering), with responsibility for maintenance of pumps, turbines, compressors, diesel engines, air conditioning and refrigeration.

Certificate of Competency (Marine Engineer Officer) – Class 2 Steamship achieved through Liverpool University.

1989–91   3rd Officer promotion

1991–present   Senior Second Officer on a tanker with responsibility for three watchkeeping personnel and training of cadets.

Instrumentation and Automatic Control Modules achieved through distance learning.

Other training courses undertaken have included firefighting, survival at sea, first aid, weapons maintenance and management.

EDUCATION HISTORY

1977–83   Harrington County Secondary School
                GCSEs gained in Maths, English Language, Physics, Geography and
                Technical Drawing.
                OND in Technology Distinction grade.

PERSONAL PROFILE

I believe that through my experience as a marine engineer I have valuable transferable skills in technical/scientific areas as well as interpersonal and leadership ability proven by my officer rank.

I am keen to pursue a challenging and responsible career, where I can build on my personal qualities and skills, and would particularly like to move into a research and development engineering role. I am committed and hardworking with an ability to work on my own initiative or as part of a team.

In my spare time I play golf and enjoy tenpin bowling. I am learning Spanish and have taught myself basic computer programming.

REFERENCES

Excellent references available on request.

This applicant was trying to career change from a job at sea to an engineering job on land by showing his transferable skills (skills he had gained at sea, which could be used in other jobs) and what he had achieved in his career through promotion and hard work.

He wanted to use this CV to elicit interest from employers in the research and development side of engineering by applying speculatively to targeted employers (which he had researched using employers' directories like *Kompass*, available in libraries) and by 'networking' (using contacts) from his career at sea. He needed to write a good covering letter to explain this new interest and to further emphasise his special skills. (See Covering Letters, pages 111–117.)

Graduate/Postgraduate Information Scientist CV

Gillian Gilligan
Radley Farm
Halton Lane
Chorton
CH4 YT7
Tel: 01876 442444

> Good profile statement to convey personality, experience and career goals

Profile

A committed, conscientious business professional with broad management experience and specific expertise in IT and training seeking a challenging role in a commercial environment.

Key Skills and Achievements

- Excellent organisational ability, working well under pressure, managing resources to meet customer requirements to deadline, as evidenced by the design, development and implementation of a PC-based administration system for Shirston Voluntary Severance Scheme
- Problem solver, using analytical, logical and innovative thinking. This has proved invaluable throughout my work experience, allowing me to be adaptable to changing situations and help identify alternative solutions to management problems.
- Achievement oriented, as proved by responsibility taken for establishment of IT section as IT manager
- Committed team player with leadership ability, demonstrated by improvement of staff morale in IT section
- Excellent written and oral communication skills with a good level of numeracy.

> Words such as 'evidenced', 'proved' and 'demonstrated' support the skills mentioned

Employment History

1997   Contract work in IT Training Services of LDT Ltd, responsible for delivery of training packages to new staff.

1995–97   Career break with only short infill contracts undertaken for Shirston.

> 'Career break' is the usual way to describe time from work to have children – no further explanation is necessary

1994–95   Shirston plc
Senior Executive Officer
Designed, developed and implemented a PC-based administration system for the company, requiring liaison with other departments to ensure the design was appropriate to all users' needs. This work had to be completed within tight deadlines and to an agreed budget, with evaluation and follow-up reports presented at board level.

1989–94   **IT Training Manager/Business Administration Manager** (same company)
After establishing the IT Training Section I was promoted as a result of career development and assumed additional responsibility for

Business Administration. This involved me in administrative support as well as personnel and financial functions, with related strategic planning and preparation of budgets.

1983–89   Arts Council
Various posts in the Library and Information Service producing briefing papers for senior management.

1983   Greater Hampton Council
As an Information Officer in the Technical Library I was involved in research and enquiry work.

1982–83   City of Hampton Polytechnic
Library Assistant (Temporary).

Membership of Professional Bodies
Associate of Institute of Personnel Development.

Vocational Training
Several inservice courses completed between 1988 and 1995 covering management, finance and marketing.

Education and Qualifications
1983   Hampton University
        MSc Information Science
1961   Wrighton University
        BSc (Hons) Environmental Management
1978   Abingley Grammar
        4 A-levels
1976   **9 O-levels**

Personal
I am a very organised and highly motivated person, both in my personal life and in my business experience. I enjoy working in a team and can perform well in a leadership role. I have good interpersonal skills and thrive on challenge and changing situations. In my spare time I enjoy fitness training, dressmaking and the breeding and showing of Shetland ponies.

References available on request.

> Interesting personal section which gives a good mix of personal qualities and interests (including the Shetland ponies, which suggests individuality!)

CHAPTER 4
Subtext and the meaning of things

'Subtext' is a term used in many ways, but for our purposes let's call it a translation of what a writer really means. For example, job adverts (see Chapter 6) are written with at least two levels of meaning:

- the superficial meaning, ie what they appear to be saying, and
- the subtext, the beneath the surface meaning, ie what the employer really wants.

Similarly, CVs and application forms are judged by the surface meaning of the words used and the articulacy of the language, but most importantly by a more subjective assessment of what is said about the applicant and what that means to the reader (the recruiter), who may be biased in any of a million ways.

The subtext of a good CV will translate something like this:

Name/Address/Tel No:	*I'm easy to contact!*
Personal profile:	*This is wonderful me and what I can offer an employer!*
Education & Qualifications:	*Look how clever I am!*
Employment experience:	*Look at what I've done!*
Relevant skills:	*This is what I'm especially good at!*
Personal/interests:	*I'm not a weird person. I do all these interesting things!*
References:	*These people will tell you how nice and wonderful I am!*

This may seem over-simplistic, but each of the sections on a CV has this kind of subtext meaning so you need to be clear about just what kind of impression you want to create.

Certain phrases and experiences are perceived as having greater value than others – for example, voluntary work is always highly rated as evidence of character and motivation; martial arts are assumed to be proof of inner strength and physical fitness; some unusual hobbies can be seen as indicative of individuality, but there is a very thin line between individualism and seeming odd!

Don't be tempted to create unusual interests to liven up your CV, but if you have a genuine interest in something and it reflects well on you, it should probably be on your CV. (Nonetheless, I have an irrational and somewhat stereotypical view that trainspotting or believing in alien encounters might be better omitted from a CV.)

Apart from this curious matter of the subtext (and I recommend that you look at every sentence on the CV and analyse 'What do I really mean?'), I would suggest that no time is wasted on woolly phrases or 'grey', weak words. Essentially what this means is that extraneous, diluted, lacklustre words must be ruthlessly eliminated to create a leaner, more concise, but effective document. Those words that are used should be powerful, conveying all your strengths. In particular the verbs chosen can make a CV work better than anything because they say 'This is what I have done'.

Some companies place such importance on the words used that they use a computer program to do the initial 'sift' of CVs to pull out a 'longlist' (the stage before a shortlist) of applicants. This program is required to search for specific 'power' words, and to give you an idea of what qualify as power words, a sample list is displayed on the next page. It is not recommended to include every one of these in a CV, as it would be immensely wordy and probably lack credibility. But if the list helps you understand the kind of words that have power, it will be useful for you to think about.

Notice how these words have a resonance or a strong, positive meaning. If any of these words particularly appeal to you, it's probably because they describe who you are and what you've done – or you wish they did. But be sure to select the words that really match your personality and your experience.

CV power words

Accelerated	Established	Managed	Reduced
Achieved	Evaluated	Marketed	Regulated
Acquired	Exceeded	Mediated	Reliable
Administered	Excellence	Motivated	Reorganised
Advised	Exceptional		Reported
Ambition	Executed	Negotiated	Represented
Analysed	Expanded	Nominated	Researched
Aspired	Experience	Notable	Responsible
Assisted			
	Facilitated	Obtained	Satisfied
Budgeted	Finalised	Operated	Scheduled
Built	Financed	Opportunity	Selected
	Formulated	Organised	Simplified
Capable	Founded	Oriented	Sincerity
Clarified		Originated	Solved
Completed	Generated	Overcome	Stimulated
Conceived	Governed		Streamlined
Confidence	Graduated	Participated	Structured
Conscientious		Perceived	Substantial
Cooperated	Headed	Perfected	Succeeded
Coordinated	Helpful	Performed	Success
Created	Honest	Permanent	Supervised
	Honour	Piloted	Supported
Decided	Humour	Pioneered	
Delegated		Placed	Taught
Demonstrated	Imagination	Planned	Thorough
Dependable	Implemented	Played	Thoughtful
Designed	Improved	Popular	Tolerant
Determined	Improvised	Practical	Trained
Developed	Increased	Praise	Transferred
Devised	Influenced	Prepared	Transformed
Displayed	Ingenuity	Prestige	Trebled
Directed	Integrity	Produced	
Distinctive	Initiated	Proficient	Understanding
Doubled	Innovated	Progress	Useful
	Inspired	Promoted	Utilised
Educated		Proposed	
Effected	Launched	Proved	Verified
Effective	Led	Provided	Vital
Efficient	Liaised	Punctual	Vivid
Encouraged	Located		
Engineered	Loyal	Reasonable	Wisdom
Enhanced		Recognised	Won
Enthusiasm	Maintained	Recommend	Wrote

Think of these words as the seasoning in a recipe which adds special flavour – don't be heavy-handed or try to use them all. You should be able to find some words in the list to help you create phrases in a CV that truly apply to you and that you feel comfortable with.

Companies that use word sifting programs generally have huge numbers of applicants and it is a quick way of screening out the dross. The second sift is normally done by humans, and this is still a 'longlist' procedure. To longlist or shortlist recruiters normally stick strictly to the criteria decided for the post as advertised (the job description – what the job involves, and the person specification – the kind of person required for the job) and try to measure how well applicants match the job specification. Those who score highly in this assessment have the best chance of reaching interview stage.

To illustrate this type of longlisting matching, a typical longlisting table is reproduced below for various candidates for a bookselling graduate vacancy. This shows how recruiters formulate the criteria for a given job (see top line of table) and then assess, as objectively as possible, how well applicants match these specifications. It underlines how important it is for an applicant to show analysis of the job description and suitability for the job as advertised (see Demystifying job adverts, pages 53–61.)

Job applied for: Bookseller/buyer with large retail group

Recruiter's longlisting criteria / Applicants	Degree HND	Other quals	Breadth of experience	Quality of letter matching the needs of the job	Skills shown in application and evidence	Other relevant comments by recruiter
Smith	BA 2:2 Kent English	MA Lit Studies	Part-time sales in student bookshop	Fair	Mention of interest in reading	Possible
Simpson ①	HND Business Studies		Library asst experience	Good	Two fluent languages	Possible
Allen	BSc 2:1 Biology	Poetry Award winner	Book warehouse vacation experience	A poor letter	People skills from all types of jobs	Possible

Henry	BA 2:2 Social Studies	Law course	Care work experience	Not a convincing letter	No skills identified	Mediocre applicant
Marshall	BA Museum Studies 1st class Hons		Very little if any work experience	Two-page endless letter!	No evidence of interest or enthusiasm for job	A pity, but seems totally unsuitable
Jones ②	BA 2:2 Open Univ Psych	Book- selling exams	Substantial retail experience	Very interesting letter, fluent/ articulate	Communication skills References from retail bookstores	Good applicant

It's fairly easy to guess which applicants scored well in this procedure, especially the ones marked 1 and 2, who were given positive remarks throughout. From this longlist, a shortlist will be created of those who may be called for a first stage of the interview procedure.

Skills and abilities – the CV minefield

Most people when asked to list their skills and abilities generally find themselves mumbling incomprehensibly or wanting to shrivel up and die. This may have something to do with the appearance of modesty many of us subscribe to, which prevents us from simply stating what we are good at. For anyone entering the jobmarket or looking for a change of career this kind of false modesty is a paralysing handicap. Very few recruiters have mystical powers, let alone the time to develop them, so unless applicants can lay out concisely and clearly what they have to offer by way of personality, skills and abilities, they are at a severe disadvantage.

Once started with this kind of self-analysis, most people find it easier than expected, so a possible fun way to start is what I call the 'Back-of-a-postage-stamp self-analysis trip' or a 'CV in a nutshell'.

Back-of-a-postage-stamp self-analysis trip

This is how it works. Let's say Humpty-Dumpty wanted to write a CV about himself and couldn't think of a thing to say; what if he had to write it on the back of a postage stamp? It would mean he could

just squeeze in: one personality characteristic
one skill
one ability
the type of job he wants.

It might look something like this:

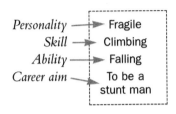

Personality ⟶ Fragile
Skill ⟶ Climbing
Ability ⟶ Falling
Career aim ⟶ To be a stunt man

It would be an extremely minimalist CV, but there really is not a lot to go on when it comes to Humpty-Dumpty. Try doing the back-of-a-postage-stamp CV with friends – you'll find it a useful exercise. What you will find is that when restricted to thinking of just one personality characteristic, one skill (something you've learned how to do), one ability (something you can do because of the person you are), your mind breaks free and throws up other attributes, so decisions have to be made to narrow the categories down to just one of each.

What it makes you do is decide, in a nutshell:

- What am I like?
- What is my main skill?
- What is my main ability?
- What do I really want?

This undiluted version of you is very potent and can be the basis of a very good CV, but keep a note of all the other skills, abilities and characteristics that crowd your mind as a result of this paring down exercise, because they will also be vital to creating the picture of you in your CV.

Another exercise to gain self-awareness of this kind is something I call 'The automatic writing trick', which tries to tap into your self-conscious and overrule your conscious, often more negative side.

The automatic writing trick

Try this… Take a blank piece of paper and a pen. You are going to write down anything that comes into your mind, most especially your hopes, dreams, aspirations and perceptions of yourself. Set a timer for three minutes and start writing immediately, as fast as you can without stopping to think, without worrying about spelling or sentence structure – write as if it is the last thing you will ever write, letting your hand scribble constantly until the timer buzzes.

Take a breath once you have finished and read what you have written; you should see some things that you expect and some that surprise you, if you have truly let your unconscious speak. It should feel quite exhilarating. This technique can be used for personal growth and development, but it can also help you with your CV preparation. Highlight words, phrases or career goals that appear and think about how to use this little piece of enlightenment.

What employers want

Of course it is useful to learn what skills, abilities and characteristics are valued by employers, just to see whether it is worth mentioning that bungee-jumping skill on a CV, so below is a list of the most desirable personal qualities, skills and abilities. You're bound to find some of yours listed – use it to jog your memory.

All-time best qualities, skills and abilities

PERSONALITY

Self-motivated	Reliable	Responsible
Imaginative	Resourceful	Common sense
Self-confident	Cooperative	Courteous
Forward thinking	Flexible	Self-reliant

SKILLS

Creativity	Numeracy	Literacy
Teamwork	Social skills	Quick to learn
Quick to grasp new ideas	Communication	Oral expression
	Problem solving	Planning/organisation
Leadership	Computer literacy	Analytical
Time management	Research skills	Presentation skills

ABILITIES

Commercial awareness	Ability to think on feet
Decision-making	Self-management/development
Ability to work under pressure	Ability to work in target-driven environment

Increasingly employers are looking for work-related transferable skills in addition to qualifications. That means any kind of work experience, whether long term, short term or voluntary, can provide an opportunity to gain valuable skills. Make a careful analysis of everything you have done to avoid overlooking vital skills. Competence is the key to employability, and if you can show your competencies, your skills and abilities, employers will fight to offer you good employment opportunities.

It is interesting to see how employers actually prioritise the skills and abilities applicants might offer, so the list below displays their top 21. Again, it is important to note how personality characteristics like willingness to learn and commitment are rated higher than more sophisticated attributes!

The top 21 skills and abilities

1. Willingness to learn
2. Commitment
3. Dependability/reliability
4. Self-motivation
5. Teamwork
6. Communication skills (spoken and written)
7. Drive/energy
8. Self-management
9. Achievement oriented/motivation
10. Problem-solving skills
11. Analytical ability
12. Flexibility
13. Initiative
14. Ability to summarise key issues
15. Logic/reasoning ability

16. Adaptability
17. Numerical skills
18. Ability to work under pressure
19. Time management
20. Research skills
21. Self-confidence.

What's amazing about this list is how possible it is for applicants to possess many of these skills and abilities. The problem is more likely to be:

- whether they are sufficiently self-aware to realise that they have them or at least a selection of them
- whether they have the confidence to display them on a CV or application form
- whether they can show *evidence* of them through work experience, study projects, voluntary work etc.

It is never going to be striking to state on an application form *'I have good time management skills'* because, of course, anyone could say that. However, if someone writes:

'In working for two different employers I have to use excellent time management and organisation skills to bring projects in according to deadlines and within budgetary targets. Both employers have awarded me "marketing assistant of the month" this year'

then there is clear evidence on offer to back up the statement.

Along with this vital 'E' for evidence on CVs and application forms, add another 'E' for enthusiasm. Many applicants are so preoccupied with creating a logical, impressive CV that they forget to show enthusiasm for what they are doing and for what they hope to do. While it would be unusual to feel enthusiastic about everything on a CV, a dose of enthusiasm, especially in the Personal section, is recommended, as enthusiasm in this often jaded, cynical world is both infectious and irresistible.

CHAPTER 5

How to do it – the blueprint for a brilliant CV

Having asked you to see a CV as a jelly mould and a postage stamp, I now want you to stretch your mind a little further to the idea of a CV as a favourite recipe. Everyone makes a cake with the same basic ingredients, but most people adapt or customise the recipe by adding an extra ingredient or individual finishing touch. Similarly, the skeleton CV, or fundamental ingredients, will consist of standard sections, but the order, format, style and any individual additions will be down to personal judgement and circumstances. For example, a college leaver with little employment experience might add a section on 'Voluntary Activities'. Some people with a 'thin' education history might equally bulk up the CV with voluntary work or particular achievements; others might add sections for training undertaken or professional qualifications gained.

The order of the sections is not set in stone, although most start with name and address and finish with Personal/Hobbies/Interests. In particular the education and employment sections can be switched around depending on the type of applicant. It is most important to hit the reader with the best first and finish with a flourish – if the first part is dull or insignificant, the reader might stop reading before getting to the impressive bit. It is common to have a self-marketing/ personal profile statement as the first item after the name and address and, at some point in the CV, a block outlining key skills.

The CV skeleton

Name, Address, Telephone Number
Self-Marketing Statement eg A wonderful, fragile egg with climb-
  ing ability and adventurous spirit, looking for work as a stunt man
Education and Qualifications or **Education History**

Career History or **Employment History** or **Work Experience**
Key Skills and Achievements (often third section of CV)
Personal/Hobbies/Interests ('I am' statements giving two or three
    key personality points and spare-time interests)
References (normally two, one personal and one work/academic).

CV Planner Extraordinaire – the blueprint

By completing the questionnaire format below you should have all
you need to create a winning CV, while the questionnaire itself helps
with the 'How do I actually do it' feeling by taking it stage by stage.
It really is a foolproof way to write a CV!

NAME	*This should be easy!*

ADDRESS

TELEPHONE NUMBER

EDUCATION HISTORY
List senior schools and colleges/universities with qualifications gained. Place date alongside each school/college/university, normally starting at the present (the most recent) and working backwards.

Date	**School/College**	**Qualifications**

KEY SKILLS AND ACHIEVEMENTS
Think of any life or work experience skills you have and list them here, along with any achievements. Try to think of three or four key skills.

1.
2.
3.
4.

EVIDENCE OF SKILLS, ACHIEVEMENTS, QUALIFICATIONS
This could be certificates, awards or commendations/references.

EMPLOYMENT/CAREER HISTORY
List work history with dates and names of employers in reverse chronology (starting most recently and working backwards). Strict forward chronology (starting in the past and working forwards) should only be used for those with little work experience, eg a new college/school leaver. Whichever method is chosen, it should be used consistently through CV. Don't forget voluntary, student or temporary work.

Dates   **Place of Work**   **Type of work and special duties**

PERSONAL/HOBBIES/INTERESTS
Think of how someone else would describe you. Ask someone close to you for three adjectives that describe you. Write them here:

1 _____   2 _____   3 _____

Now how would you describe yourself, if different to the above:

1 _____   2 _____   3 _____

What are you like in a work situation, eg reliable, conscientious...?

List any hobbies or interests here

CAREER OBJECTIVE
Try to write a statement about yourself, what kind of person you are, using good strong adjectives (see section before and 'CV power words' for ideas) and detailing the kind of work you are seeking, something like:
A _____, _____ (two adjectives) person or name of job title, with strong _____ (key skills) skills looking for _____ (type of work sought). For example:
*An **enthusiastic, positive** youth worker with **leadership and counselling** skills, seeking **work with young offenders**.*

How to actually write the CV

1. Decide on the order you wish to use for the sections (see CV skeleton on the previous pages). You should start with Name and Address and end with a Personal and References section. Education and Employment sections can be swapped around depending on the type of applicant.
   Place the Career Objective underneath the block heading with Name, Address and Telephone number.

2. Use evidence of skills and abilities to bring to life duller sections.

3. Use 'I' statements to personalise CV and give a real feeling of a living, breathing person behind the document (eg '**I am** able to work under pressure').

4. Place Key Skills section where it will give maximum effect – eg boxed at the top, underneath name and address.

5. Use simple, real language and avoid jargon.

6. Don't feel you have to give a detailed explanation of every job function – focus on key areas; leave out explanations for jobs of lesser importance, or where the job title says it all, eg Pub Glass Collector.

7. Check that the formatting works to your advantage and decide on font style, layout etc.

8. Move sections around to see what looks best.

9. Keep it to two pages; if necessary do a separate references page or just write 'References available on request'.

10. Write it, wordprocess it and then put it away for a day or two. Then go back and read it and decide if it works for you. Does it make sense and convey a real impression of you?

11. *Finally, check for the three 'L's and the two 'E's:*
    Is the **layout** perfect?
    Is it **logical**?
    Is it **lively** (alive)?
    Have you expressed **enthusiasm**?
    Is there **evidence** for skills and experience?

What do you do with a CV?

This might seem a little obvious but, apart from applying for advertised vacancies that request a CV, there are a few other – often better – ways of using a CV. The fact is that a huge number of jobs are **never advertised**, so waiting for the job you want to be advertised may be a fruitless business.

As a little exercise, pick a sample of ten of your friends and ask them how they found their jobs; you may discover that half of them are working as a result of contacts, often referred to as 'networking', or from having contacted particular firms speculatively, often referred to as 'on the off chance'.

So if you want to access the obvious and hidden jobmarkets you need to use various strategies, and your CV can play an important part in this more innovative jobsearch.

Some other-than-obvious ways to use a CV

- Target employers that you have researched. Look at who is advertising regularly in the field that interests you and use business directories in libraries to learn about good employers.
- Give copies of your CV to friends who work for companies that interest you. Ask them to gauge interest from various departments, then follow up with phone calls, asking for an informal chat about possible openings.
- Take a CV with you to meetings or interviews with employers and leave as a calling card/memory jogger to keep you in their minds.
- Send a one-page résumé CV ahead of a meeting, and take the fuller, two-page version with you.
- Phone round speculatively to employers and, if they say they don't have openings, ask if they could afford the time to look at your CV and give any advice (you could either send a copy or meet them to go through it). It is quite surprising how helpful people can be, if their advice is sought, and they may be able to come up with other firms for you to contact.
- Make sure you write a good covering letter to accompany the

CV, drawing attention to particular features of your CV (see Chapter 10 on covering letters).

These are some of the useful things you can do with your CV. If you have given yourself the chance to absorb the variety of CV styles in this first section, and follow the blueprint formula, you should be able to create a winning CV which is a vital, positive step in a positive jobsearch strategy or career change. There is nothing to stop you now – so get going!

CHAPTER 6 Demystifying job adverts through psychoanalysis

The best thing to learn

Don't be tempted to skip this chapter – it could be a big mistake. Once learned, the expertise of job advert psychoanalysis can transform the way you apply for jobs and improve your success rate by 100%. That may seem a grand claim, but think back to the way you viewed TV adverts as a child. Remember before disillusionment set in, when you took all adverts at face value? Of course you believed that MegaKleano would remove chocolate stains and leave your T-shirts soft, and that eating Shuggersnax was a healthy and nutritious way to stay full until lunchtime

But disillusionment did set in and you began the process of sifting the information contained in the adverts for truth. Surprisingly, most adults looking at job adverts are still at that almost foetal developmental stage as far as judging, analysing and sifting for real meaning goes. Often the enticing language disables rational thought and makes some people desire the job so much that they persuade themselves they are suitable with no real justification. In contrast, for people with lack of confidence or low self-esteem the opposite occurs – the glamorous portrayal of the job terrifies them into thinking they are not gifted enough, again often with absolutely no justification.

Clearly a more discriminating approach is required to prevent the wrong applicants applying for unsuitable jobs and to ensure that less confident, but possibly perfectly adequate applicants are not dissuaded from applying for jobs through lack of clear thinking.

To a degree it is all about practice and experience; having been bombarded by TV adverts as children we learnt the skill of discerning elements of truth from the shallow surface reality. We are less practised with job adverts due to lack of opportunity, but it is simple to gain an expertise in a crash course sort of way, and anyone considering a change of career, or embarking on a job search should take the time to do this. Here's how…

Take a look at the following job adverts and, as with application forms and CVs, look first for the surface, up front, sometimes factual meaning; then imagine you are one of those comic book super-heroes, the one with X-ray eyes. Engage your power to see through the outer, fleshy bits to the skeleton of the job advert. Perhaps truth will not be revealed, but the distractions of surface glitz will be removed.

X-ray these job adverts!

Here are a random selection of typical ads, some basic, others more complex.

Advert 1

Is food your life?
Want to work for the biggest hotel group in the country?
Catering Manager
Darrow UK is dedicated to customer service and the growth of our business. This has made us a dynamic, fast-moving, successful organisation.

As a team manager, with responsibility for the catering area, you will be an outstanding communicator, a progressive thinker and a proactive individual, able to motivate and lead teams and to consistently provide a quality customer service to the highest standards.

Hospitality experience is vital, along with a background in customer service and in team work. An ambitious, achievement oriented individual, you will respond well to the challenge of working for a market leader.

Training and promotion opportunities for applicants with the right profile are excellent.

Phone 0110 105 6748 for an application pack.
Closing date: 26 November

Tooth and Co
require an experienced
DENTAL
TECHNICIAN/ASSISTANT
To include laboratory and clerical duties.
Ability to use time effectively is important as time will be allotted to lab work and office duties dealing with patients.
Dexterity and hand-eye coordination are essential.
Telephone 01200 743233 for an application form.
Training is available for less experienced but committed applicants.

Advert 2

Advert 3

Advert 4

By comparing the surface view with the X-ray view a clearer, more
rational picture of the job advert emerges and makes it easier for a
prospective applicant to decide whether it really is a suitable job for
them. Let's make these adverts take the couch in turn and we can
begin to psychoanalyse what they are really about.

Advert 1 – Catering Manager

Organisation profile	Factual Info	Subjective/Subtext Info
Biggest hotel group? Dynamic Fast moving Successful	Catering Manager. Hospitality experience (not clear at what level). Customer service experience. Team-worker with leadership skills. 'Outstanding communicator' suggests these would be key skills.	Language suggests a fairly driven organisation. Ambitious and achievement oriented. 'Progressive thinker' suggests individualistic, problem-solving streak. 'Proactive' means being ahead of the game, innovatory.
Conclusion: They want to be bigger and better	*Conclusion:* They need an experienced manager with high level skills	*Conclusion:* These are the important additional extras they are seeking and it is very difficult to prove these kind of qualities

Try scoring yourself out of ten as to how you match the above job as analysed this way. Circle skills, abilities, experience and personal qualities you could cite as evidence.

Obviously this might not be your dream job, but it is fairly typical in terms of job advert jargon, and by X-raying it you can demystify it a little by separating out the essential (Factual Info) and desirable criteria (Subjective/Subtext Info) wanted by employers. Note how adverts use assumptive language to tempt you to see yourself in the job! For longlisting purposes, employers would start by sifting for those who fulfil the essential criteria, and then shortlist the longlist by selecting those with over and above the desirable criteria. If you do not possess at least the essential criteria specified your application will be a waste of effort.

Here are the other three adverts decoded.

Advert 2 – Dental Technician/Assistant

Organisation profile	Factual Info	Subjective/Subtext Info
Small practice needs flexible, multiskilled staff	Dental Technician/Asst Training available so they would accept someone less experienced than originally indicated. Mix of clerical and technical skills required.	Dexterity and hand–eye coordination are difficult to assess without giving a manual dexterity test. Dealing with patients implies interpersonal skills. Good time-management and being able to work on own initiative are implied here

Advert 3 – Office Administrator

Organisation profile	Factual Info	Subjective/Subtext Info
Small, busy firm	Office Administrator Excellent computer skills and confident telephone manner needed.	Organisational skills and ability to work to deadlines will need to be proved.

Advert 4 – IT Adviser/PC Support

Organisation profile	Factual Info	Subjective/Subtext Info
Leading building contractor? Very strong IT use	IT Adviser/PC Support Basic IT experience in user support and networking	Communication and problem solving are key skills required

What this psychoanalysis emphasises is that if the advert can be visualised in a more elemental way, the key qualities, skills, abilities and experience required can be easily identified.

- The **organisation profile** can help you determine if the company ethos suits you; whether you would prefer a large, medium or small set-up, whether a target-driven or more laid-back environment suits you.

- The **factual information** helps you decide if you fit the basic requirements set down by the employer and you will need to have evidence to back this up.

- The **subjective/subtext information** demands that you have a clear picture of your key strengths developed through experience and/or qualifications and that you are self-aware enough of your personal gifts and talents.

How to check if you really match the job you are applying for

It is worth using the template on the next page to analyse job adverts and ensure you get to grips with what they are really about. If you score highly when you match yourself against the job, it is certainly worth applying, and you have the basic framework for completing a winning application form.

Once you have analysed a job advert and filled in the organisation profile, the factual information and the subjective information, do a similar analysis of yourself and match the answers, comparing them against the job requirements. Give yourself a score out of ten as to how well you match the job. Use details from the 'ME' section when you fill out application forms to justify your suitability for jobs.

JOB/PERSON MATCH

Complete the sections below by analysing a job advert	Complete the sections below with an analysis of your own personal qualities, skills, abilities and experience
JOB ADVERT...	**ME...**
Organisation profile	Personal qualities
Factual information	Skills
Subjective/subtext information	Abilities
Score out of ten for match between job advert and ME	Experience

In many cases employers send out an application pack to people who respond to the job advert. These usually have more detailed information about the job and their requirements. Be aware that the more detailed the information provided by an employer, the more that will be expected of individuals to justify their application.

A similar approach can be used to the job advert psychoanalysis. On the next page are details of a job vacancy provided in an application pack, with the decoded message on the right.

Normally two main documents will be supplied, a job description and a person or personnel specification. The job description is (rather obviously) a description of the job, often written in somewhat formal, even inaccessible language, and this needs to be decoded or stripped down to be of any real use to an applicant.

The person specification is a description of the kind of person required for the job – that is, the employer's dream applicant!

A decoded job description

BAMPTON HOSPITAL
JOB DESCRIPTION

Job title: Medical Records Clerk

General responsibilities: To provide an efficient clerical support to the medical and nursing staff.

Key Duties	Decoded
1. Clinic preparation	*Organised,*
2. Case note filing and preparation	*attention to detail,*
3. Maintenance of patient records	*confidentiality important.*
4. Registration of new patients and amendment of existing ones	*Polite, sociable, good at dealing with people.*
5. Efficient tracing of all case notes	*Ability to work under pressure*
6. Correspondence with outside agencies	*Telephone work, communication skills*
7. Participate in In-Service training scheme	*Willing to be trained.*
8. To deal with computer back-up procedures when necessary	*IT skills and*
9. To report to the Medical Records Officer any apparent or suspected fault with the data displayed on the VDU	*problem-solving.*
10. To observe the requirements of the Data Protection Act 1984.	

This is just a straightforward analysis of the job description, taking into account factual information and a reasonable, subjective assessment of what the employer is implying, decoded or translated into more specific language, by way of phrases, which can be then used on the application form.

Now let's take a look at the corresponding person specification, which has been annotated by the applicant (see italics) with relevant details. Additionally, the applicant has matched her view of herself to the person specification by a ticking system, and added her own notes at the bottom,

Person specification demystified

Post: Clerk   **Dept:** Medical Records

	Essential	**Desirable**
Physical	Good health, normal hearing & vision Neat, tidy appearance	Over 18 years ✓
Education/training Job experience	General education to GCSE standard or equivalent	GCSE pass or equivalent in English Language ✓ Some office experience
General intelligence *[Being able to work on my own or as part of a team]*	Initiative/motivation to work without supervision	Able to work with varied groups of staff ✓
Special aptitudes Interests	Attention to detail ✓ Some outside interests *[Volunteer work will be relevant – visiting elderly people]*	Previous VDU experience
Disposition Self-reliance *[Hardworking, responsible, caring]*	Able to get on well as a team member Reliable Conscientious Punctual Helpful & sympathetic	Cheerful Able to work under pressure ✓
Circumstances *[Recent evening classes to update wordprocessing skills]*	Able to work hours stated Willing to train in other Records Sections	Easy travel to and from work

Proof of personal qualities – References – Voluntary work
Proof of skills – Teamwork through previous employment – Responsibility and own initiative through voluntary work

By collating the notes from the company's job description and person specification, this applicant found it a very easy process to complete the application form corresponding to that employer's requirements, and was able to produce a thorough, considered and person-centred application.

So remember that, to create a winning application, you have to be prepared to put in some work on the job advert and application form details to give yourself the best chance of succeeding. In fact, it's better than a chance, it's a foregone conclusion that you will succeed if you go about it in a systematic way.

Nonetheless, it will not matter how much work is done on the job advert or description if you are not prepared to disclose things about yourself or if you have not spent time analysing who you really are and what you have to offer (see 'Back-of-a-postage-stamp self-analysis trip', page 42). Being over-modest makes you your own worst enemy, because if the employer is saying, in either a mysterious or obvious way, 'This is what I have to offer', you must be prepared to return the favour.

It really is very simple to engage in this process. Reluctance to analyse yourself is like sticking doggedly to that basic cake recipe and not having the individuality or enthusiasm to make it different and better by adding your own personal touch.

Rest assured that only good can come from it – self-knowledge is a valuable skill and will benefit you in every area of your life.

CHAPTER 7

Application forms – from caterpillar to butterfly

Application forms appeal to the part of many of us that craves a refuge from chaos. So often we throw ourselves at them eagerly, as if by fitting ourselves into these small spaces we will be made whole – our lives will fit neatly into the boxes with nothing to spare and, by performing this orderly process, we will obtain the ultimate reward, the job of our dreams. Of course, nothing that magic can happen as a result of some scribbling in boxes, and for many the experience becomes more like a black hole, as we are sucked into a dark void and never return to tell the tale. Perhaps our expectations are simply too high; nonetheless, after a couple of failures, or even near misses, all we remember about application forms is the black hole feeling.

Let's call this the worst case scenario, but even the less awful cases can be fairly damaging to our confidence, so it's time to take away from the application form its power to paralyse, stultify and shine a bright light on our flaws; forget the application form as a black hole – think of it as a cutlery tray!

Picture a cutlery tray in your kitchen drawer; could anything be more innocuous? Without labels to help us, we manage to put forks, knives and spoons in their proper places. While it's true that some people may jumble all the cutlery up and ignore the sections, most of us know how to deal with a cutlery tray – you just put the right things in the right sections as neatly as possible. In essence it is exactly the same for application forms...

Put things in the right places as neatly as possible!

This may seem like an over-simplification, but if only *this* is done perfectly, you achieve virtually a winning application. However, as this is essentially so easy to accomplish, it is possible to do just a tiny bit more and be transformed. By that I mean see yourself uniquely displayed in the application form frame in all your glory. Let's see what all this means by looking at three stages of application forms, from ugly little caterpillar to chrysalis to butterfly.

Caterpillar application form – half-hearted and nothing quite right

Please complete grey sections in block capitals in black ink.	
Name *Ben Cameron* **Address** *Pie Cottage,* *Bun Lane, Rabbiton, Norfolk* **Tel** *01987 665434* **Date of Birth** *6/6/98*	**Post applied for** *Office Assistant* **Company** **Where advertised**
Education　　　　**Dates** *St Mary's High School 1990–96*	**Qualifications** *GCSE Maths, Art and Drama*
Employment Experience *School work experience 1995* *Plunkett and Co*	**Hobbies and Interests** *Golf, shooting and fishing*
Any other relevant information to support your application	**Please give names and addresses of two referees** *Mr Harold Smith* *3 Sad Lane, Holesworth* *Norfolk*
Signature	**Date** *10/9/98*

This is a fairly basic application form completed in a fairly basic style; the simplicity of the form itself is its prime danger. First, let's look at the common, rather obvious mistakes, which even rather clever people are prone to make:

1. **Read the instructions.** Block capitals are requested for basic personal details (grey section), and here they have been ignored.

2. **Date of birth is incorrect.** This is a very common error (frequently on university applications) and implies that applicants are applying prenatally.

3. **Where advertised.** Employers are interested in where you heard about their vacancy, so they can review which publicity/advertising is the best value; it is a courtesy to help them with this. Leaving it blank shows lack of attention to detail.

4. **Big open white spaces** on forms are to be avoided, so giving as much detail as possible is vital. Grades should normally be specified for exam qualifications (especially for recent graduates or school-leavers; mid-career grades are less important, so play them down if they weren't too good). Any other alternative qualifications can and ought to be added, eg, First Aid, Driving Test passed etc, where space allows.

5. **Thin employment experience** ought to be expanded; details of the type of work undertaken would at least add interest.

6. **Full sentences** in the Hobbies and Interests section would add a little eloquence and perhaps some idea of personality, for example, 'In my spare time I enjoy golf, shooting and fishing and would describe myself as an outdoor sort of person.'

7. **Any other relevant information** is the ideal place to show enthusiasm for the work applied for and to mention any key skills and abilities. Leaving this blank suggests lack of enthusiasm or a rushed application or, worst, that you have nothing to offer.

8. **Further omissions**, only one referee detailed and no signature, a very common error, confirm this as a slipshod application.

Let's now look at the chrysalis stage of this application form.

Chrysalis application form – put things in the right places as neatly as possible

Please complete grey sections in block capitals in black ink.

Name BEN CAMERON

Address PIE COTTAGE,
BUN LANE, RABBITON,
NORFOLK N14 5PL

Tel 01987 665434

Date of Birth 6/6/79

Post applied for
OFFICE ASSISTANT

Company
PARAGON PRINTING

Where advertised
EVENING ECHO

> These sections are lined up in a much more professional way

Education   Dates

St Mary's High School 1990-96

> These sections are still a little blank. More detail would help or the information could be spread out to fill the sections

Qualifications

GCSE Maths (C), Art (B) and Drama (E)
St John's Ambulance First Aid Diplomas
at Intermediate and Advanced Level

Employment Experience

School work experience 1995
Plunkett and Co, Office Junior

Hobbies and Interests

Golf, shooting and fishing

Any other relevant information to support your application

I am very interested in office work and think that my desktop publishing skills gained from my art coursework will help me working in the office of a printing company

> Explanation of interest for type of work and knowledge of type of work offered

Please give names and addresses of two referees

Mr Harold Smith
3 Sad Lane
Holesworth
Norfolk N25 1BH

> Nicely lined up info in these sections

Mrs V Mole
43 Harring Road
Minkley
Norfolk N12 2NF

Signature Ben Cameron

Date 10/9/98

Just a bit more – the butterfly – a winning application

Please complete grey sections in block capitals in black ink.

Name BEN CAMERON
Address PIE COTTAGE,
BUN LANE, RABBITON
NORFOLK N14 5PL
Tel 01987 665434
Date of Birth 6/6/79

Post applied for
OFFICE ASSISTANT
Company
PARAGON PRINTING
Where advertised
EVENING ECHO

Education **Dates**
St Mary's High School 1990–96

Qualifications
GCSE Maths (C)
Art (B)
Drama (E)
St John's Ambulance First Aid Diplomas
at Intermediate and Advanced Level

> Better layout of qualifications

Employment Experience
School work experience 1995
Plunkett and Co, Office Junior
Main duties included photocopying,
filing, wordprocessing and checking
orders.

> Basic explanation of experience

Hobbies and Interests
I have played golf since the age of 8, and
have competed in various junior
competitions. I also enjoy shooting, fishing
and outdoor pursuits.
In other spare time I am developing a new
interest in wildlife watercolour painting.

Any other relevant information to support application
I am very interested in office work and
think that my desktop publishing skills
gained from my art coursework will help
me working in the office of a printing
company.
I have good numerical skills and feel
confident about dealing with the financial
side of office assistant work.
I am hardworking, sociable and can work
in a team or on my own initiative.

Please give names and addresses of two referees
Mr Harold Smith
3 Sad Lane
Holesworth
Norfolk N25 1BH

Mrs V Mole
43 Harring Road
Minkley
Norfolk N12 2NF

> Interest, enthusiasm, evidence!

Signature Ben Cameron   **Date** 10/9/98

This is of course a very simple application form for a very basic level job; however, the principles of achieving good application forms are all emphasised in the three stages, summed up in this advice:

- pay attention to instructions and details
- stress marketable skills and qualities
- match the application form to the requirements of the employer
- be enthusiastic and give evidence where possible of what you have to offer.

The mind of the application form writer

It is said that a crossword can reveal the mind of its compiler, and similarly each application form design has a character of its own and shows quite clearly the (possibly twisted) mind of the writer. Each employer has their own agenda when it comes to recruiting staff, often known as the 'general and specific criteria'.

THE GENERAL CRITERIA
Those qualities desirable in **all** prospective employees, according to the demands of that company.

THE SPECIFIC CRITERIA
Those qualities desirable or even essential for that company and that particular job.

Given these aspects and the fact that many forms are carefully crafted to highlight certain criteria of applicants, it's a bit irritating for an employer when sections of the form are, misconstrued or ignored. In some cases it can be the fault of the application form and its creator if prospective candidates misunderstand instructions or headings because they are obscure or simply baffling. However, it has to be said that in the majority of cases it is the strange reluctance of applicants to **read** the form that causes mistakes.

We all lead busy lives and non-essential reading is often avoided, so that the artless simplicity of the application form tempts us with the familiar self-indulgent whisper of '*I can fill in the boxes without reading it first – I know what is needed here'*. This is the one and only trap on an application form – the over-confident/don't want to read it/bored with it already trap, and it is lethal! Everyone knows that it makes sense to read through the whole form first, before putting pen to paper, but only a few meticulous souls do it.

Make a promise to yourself that you will *read*, not just scan the form and you will increase your chances of success immeasurably. Now I'm going to teach you how to read it thoroughly, just in case it's not entirely clear!

How to read and prepare to complete an application form like a professional

Do a surface scan of the form and find out the following.

1. What precise instructions are there?

These could be minimal and basic like 'Use block capitals through-out' or 'Write in black pen' or they could be far more detailed, for example:

'Sapphire Holdings uses a candidate tracking system and would recom-mend the following to applicants:

- *Handwrite the application in clear, legible writing, as the form will be copied and reduced in size*
- *Emphasise key skills in relation to the job specification supplied*
- *Avoid using jargon or abbreviations.'*

Make a separate note of these instructions to fix them in your mind!

2. What size are the main sections on the form?

For most sections a set amount of space is allocated, which gives a clue as to how much you should write, so it is a good idea to adjust your wordage to the size of the sections, always resisting the tempta-tion to waffle just to fill the space!

Try measuring a section and work out how many words in your normal handwriting it will take to fill it, and when working on the final draft bear this in mind – remembering that brevity is generally the key to dynamic and effective language (Compare some well-known words such as *'Let there be light!'* to an alternative, less concise version which might have gone something like: *'It would be a really good idea if there was some light here to show my great creativity and total power over the universe'*.)

Communication ability is one of the skills employers most frequently demand. The best proof of this on an application form is the use of effective language; the way sections are completed, making the most of space allotted, with concise, precise language, is an obvious corroboration of these skills.

3. What size is the final Personal Statement section?

This section often trips up the unwary by allowing applicants the opportunity to continue on another page (for example *'Please continue on a separate page, if necessary.'*) This may be viewed as a good judgement/decision-making trap, although employers probably do not intend it that way. This is how it entraps in its highly innocent way:

■ Should you risk leaving something important out?
■ Ought you to crunch up writing to fit something in?
■ Should you start another page and run out of steam (or rather anything interesting to say)?
■ Should you waffle on to fill another page?
■ Or will taking an extra page mean that you enrich and enlarge on personal skills and abilities with enthusiasm and evidence?

It has to be said that in most cases when an extra page is opted for, information is repeated and little is gained except the animosity of the reader, so if in doubt, it is recommended that the Personal Statement section allocated is well used, and all relevant information about the applicant's suitability is crafted into that allotted space. In most cases that space allows for about 20–30 lines of text (hand-written), or 200–300 words.

It is rare that doubling the number of words would provide an improved version, but if someone has wide employment experience and excellent communication skills, or where a very detailed personal statement is demanded by the recruiter, it is possible, with preparation and planning, to do this well (see how to write a dynamic Personal Statement, pages 80–83). So do use good judgement on this section and remember the power of a few words well phrased. (Consider JF Kennedy's memorable quote *'Ich bin ein Berliner'*, when he could have said *'I feel lots of solidarity and kinship with the Berlin people and I'm really glad to be here!'* He would never have been remembered for the second version, but he added to history with the first.)

4. What image is conveyed about the employer by the application form, and does your personality fit with the corporate ethos this suggests?

This may seem irrelevant, but if something or everything about the application form or job description/application pack does not feel right to you, it may be worth asking why this is. A good, objective, well-ordered application form reflects a good employer as much as a biased, confusing one implies a bad one. Be confident enough to trust your instincts and exercise the right to boycott an employer if inappropriate or biased questions are asked; this may seem idealistic but it may save you some pain at a later stage.

Journey to below the surface

Having analysed the job description and person specification (see Chapter 6 on how to psychoanalyse a job advert), both in the job advert and in the recruitment information, you will have a list of personality qualities, skills, abilities and possibly interests needed for the job.

Start with a mental exercise

With the job advert psychoanalysis close at hand, start to analyse the application form in the same way, going through section by section, question by question, working out exactly what each box wants from you, **without writing anything.** Some sections will be objective, simple 'information only' boxes and others will have a subtext or underlying meaning, directly corresponding to the general and specific criteria desired by the employer, backed up by the job advert.

Now follow these simple steps to creating a perfect application – it may seem painstaking and even boring, but imagine someone has a gun to your head and unless you create a faultless application you will die! It does concentrate the mind a little to do the application form **as if your life depends on it**, and when your rational side balks at this over-exaggerated perspective, just say to yourself

'But my life does depend on this!'

…which of course, in a way, it does.

Below are the foolproof steps you have to take – take them one at a time and don't let boredom tempt you to rush or cut corners!

Ten steps to a heavenly application form (the first stage)

1. Photocopy the form at least twice and put the real form away in a safe place.
2. Concentrate on copy form Mark 1 and plan to know it as intimately as a fascinating acquaintance with a mysterious past.
3. **Read** the form – check it with the same intensity as you would a lottery coupon, when you suspect your numbers might have come up.
4. Scan the form and put it into one of four categories:
   - the straightforward and simple, objective type (very rare), *don't be carried away and forget to concentrate*;
   - the simple but misleading type, *take note of the tricky questions;*
   - the simple-seeming, lull you into false sense of security type, with a few final mind-numbingly complex questions, *meditate, cogitate and concentrate;*
   - the complex, objective and subjective questioning form (often for graduate jobs) – *all of the above italicised instructions should be combined together and muttered like a mantra as a vital pre-application psyche-up.*
5. Go through each box on the copy form, writing in what is really required, either **basic accurate information** or **subtext**, that is, more subjective, job specific criteria like skills/abilities.
6. In the margin write any subtext or below-the-surface meaning points you might notice.

7. Verify whether and how this subtext matches your job advert/specification analysis. Mark this subtext with an equals sign connecting in to something in the job description.
8. Check your job advert analysis for employer's requirements (personality, skills or abilities) that you can prove by way of **evidence** (uncovered, confirmed and detailed in job advert psychoanalysis process), and in red pen annotate sections with what the employer wants and how you can demonstrate your suitability.
9. Mark an intriguing, perhaps scary section with a silly symbol to defuse the terror you feel when you look at it.
10. Read the **whole form again** and check to see if you have missed anything.

You should eventually have a copy form with valuable points emphasised and a skeleton version of what you want to say, perfectly synchronised to the employer's needs, as conveyed by the form itself and the job advert/application information.

On the next page is what Copy Form Mark 1 should look like. Having completed Copy Form Mark 1 with as much detail and information as possible, move on to Copy Form Mark 2 (the other blank copy of the application form), as this will be the final rough draft format.

Copy Form Mark 1

Please write in block capitals in black ink.

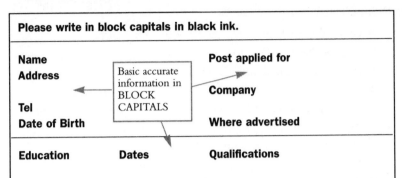

Name		Post applied for
Address		
	Basic accurate information in BLOCK CAPITALS	Company
Tel		
Date of Birth		Where advertised

Education	Dates	Qualifications

Employment experience
Skills needed – teamwork, problem-solving. Experience of customer service – remember banking experience and award.

Subtext
What experience have they suggested is desirable or essential? If you have little experience, mention vacation, part-time, casual or voluntary work.

Hobbies and interests
Extra skills – organisational from committee work and financial from fundraising.

Subtext
Are you interesting? What sort of personality do your interests suggest? Spare time commendable interests? Try not to look too busy to have time for work!

Any other relevant information to support your application
Why I want to work, what I have to offer – experience/personal qualities – positive and organised

Basic accurate information and subtext
Personal Statement information to back up application – try to convey a sense of personality, skills and abilities with evidence and enthusiasm.

Referees names and addresses

Basic accurate information
Seek permission from prospective referees and give full titles and responsibilities, eg Mr E Smith, Headmaster.

Signature   **Date**

Copy Form Mark 2 recipe (the second stage)

INGREDIENTS

- A good black pen (one that favours your handwriting)
- A good hard surface to write on
- A fine-line pencil and eraser
- Some ruled paper that can be seen through the form or the lined page of a standard letter writing pad (very few people can write straight on a form without help and this improves the appearance of the final form)
- Scrap paper to compose meaningful sentences
- All relevant information and dates of education, employment and qualifications
- Job advert psychoanalysis (see Chapter 6) with list of qualities, skills, abilities required for job, matched with what you possess, plus Copy Form Mark 1
- Your Personal Statement Draft (see Chapter 8).

METHOD

1. Read the whole form again and focus your mind.
2. Start with the information only sections and fill in basic details, using the pencil, remembering to use capitals when required, and to line up information in an orderly way. Keep lined page behind form to ensure straightness of lines of text or rule in faint pencil lines to ensure straightness of text; lines can be erased on final copy.
3. Complete Personal Statement (see how to write a Personal Statement in Chapter 8) maintaining paragraph sections and ensuring evenness and consistency of handwriting. (Some people have a tendency to swap handwriting style from upright to sideways or backwards slant as they write, and this results in a messy appearance.) Make sure positive/power words (as suggested on page 40) are used to best effect.
4. Fill in subtext type boxes, remembering to add anything not mentioned elsewhere and to avoid repetition.
5. Squint up your eyes and view the finished draft. Check the surface look. Erase any errors, line up text, check the details against job analysis and Copy Form Mark 1.

6. If possible, leave the draft for 24 hours and then return to it and check for articulacy of language, attention to detail, the match of application to job advertised, evidence of skills and abilities and, lastly, enthusiasm. Ask someone really 'picky' to check spellings and punctuation. If it all makes sense and looks good and reads well, then complete the actual form in an identical way using the very good black pen.

FINISHING TOUCHES
Post in an A4 envelope to maintain pristine appearance!

Less straightforward application forms and how to handle them

There are as mentioned before many styles and types of application form, and having looked at a very simple, basic one it is worth considering the next stage in evolution, the apparently simple form with the odd tricky questions.

A very ordinary application form (the most misleading kind)

Application for the post of

Surname

Forename

Address

Telephone No (Home)

Date of Birth

> Basic information sections

Previous Employment

Employer   From   To   Post details

> Brief details of main duties of posts are needed here – emphasise relevant experience corresponding to job applied for, so that you show you have read the job specification and believe you can fulfil the essential and desirable criteria for the job.

Education

(Details of secondary schools and colleges attended)

Schools/Colleges   From   To   Qualifications obtained

> Start with most recent qualifications and work backwards; if space allows detail grades achieved.

Details of any other relevant training, qualifications or experience

> Make sure any additional training or qualifications are given here, including part-time study, distance learning or in-company short courses undertaken. Relate additional training to job applied for. Try not to leave this blank! The subtext to this section is saying 'What else have you got to offer?'

Personal Section
Please complete this section, detailing interests and personal skills, which might support your application.

> THE SHOOT YOURSELF IN THE FOOT SECTION!
> A logical, considered format is needed here to convey exactly what you have to offer and why the employer must shortlist you for interview. It is the application form version of a sales pitch – it does not just promise – it delivers!
>   You don't have to reinvent yourself but you do have to focus on the key strengths and skills you have that will interest this employer.
>   Clues as to how this section should be completed are hidden in the above statement, so work out a format that covers the three sections mentioned: interests – your interest in the type of work offered and any other related interests; personal qualities – those relevant to the job particularly; key skills which you possess directly related to the job.
>   Support this with evidence by way of previous work experience or study undertaken and finish with a concluding self-description and assumptive statement, for example, 'I am a positive, hardworking, motivated person and all these qualities I will bring to the post of sales manager.'

Give the names and addresses of two referees below

> Think carefully about who you ask to be referees – they really must hold you in high regard!

> So many people forget to sign and date application forms – it's so obvious but is such a common error.

Signature   Date

How to match a typical job advert to this very ordinary application form

Let's take a look at the process of creating an application form that is synchronised to the job advert and answers all the implied questions the advert asks.

The advert and the implied questions that need to be answered

> **Halliwell Greetings Cards plc**
> **Hall Street, Newton N56 7RT**
> **Product Planner**
> This is an exciting opportunity to join our Marketing team where you will be responsible for planning and control of an extensive range of product lines.
> You will use excellent communication skills to liaise with retailers, merchandisers and sales staff and be expected to produce evaluation reports on product performance for future market planning.
> A high level of numeracy is essential. You will also be computer literate, working well in a team and on your own initiative. An interest in greeting cards, particularly humorous, is essential.
> Application forms available from...

Find out anything you can about the company. Try phoning up and asking for a company report.

Marketing degree and/or experience is implied here.

Skills clearly demanded are communication, customer service, report writing, numeracy, teamwork and leadership.

Sense of humour might be useful!

Now take a look at the application form to match this job.

Application for Product Planner

Application for the post of *PRODUCT PLANNER*
Surname   *ALLEN*
Forename   *JACK*
Address   *13 PEACOCK ROAD,*
                                           SUNLEY, S67 Y78
Telephone No (Home)   *01989 567432*
Date of Birth   *9 SEPTEMBER 1972*

Previous Employment

Employer	From	To	Post details
Marvellous Mags, Hapton	*1995*	*present*	*Marketing and Promotions Manager Responsible for advertising revenue with promotion of 30 magazines to major news retailers*
Paragon Printing	*1993*	*1995*	*Marketing and Sales Assistant, including initial training as part of sales team, followed by target marketing of magazine customers, resulting in 80% circulation increase*

Paragon Printing Sunley	1990	1993	Admin assistant in advertising dept dealing with telesales, accounts and stock control

Education

Schools/Colleges	From	To	Qualifications obtained
Sunley College Marketing modules	1988	1990	BTec Business Administration with . Distinction gained
Sunley High	1983	1988	GCSEs in Maths (A), English (B), Business Studies (B), Science (C) History (B)

Details of any other relevant training, qualifications of experience

1992 Achieved merit grade in City & Guilds Information Technology course through part-time study
1994 Gained accreditation through Institute of Marketing via distance learning
1995 Leadership training undertaken through in-company initiative run by Motivate Management Consultancy

Personal Section
Please complete this section, detailing interests and personal skills which might support your application.

I have wanted to work for Halliwell Greeting Cards since I read an article in Marketing Today about its campaign to raise finance for ecological projects through its extensive recycling initiatives.

I want to work in Product Planning as I feel I have the right background and experience to fulfil the requirements of the job; most recently I have been involved in evaluating retail customer requirements and promoting new and often less popular lines with considerable success. A recent success has been the increase in sales of a new fishing magazine, which was promoted via mailshots and special offers to fishing clubs and shops, with sponsorship of a local young fisherman.

I have broad experience (from the ground upwards) in marketing and in consequence am adaptable and multiskilled enough to lead by example as a marketing manager; I am computer literate and familiar with spreadsheet and finance packages connected with the printing industry, and have communication skills both as a previous sales trainee and through dealing with customers

I am extrovert, confident and enthusiastic and can use my sense of humour to defuse stressful situations, where appropriate. I would be happy to give evidence of any of the above qualities, skills or abilities at interview or through an assessed presentation.

Give the names and addresses of two referees below

Someone to vouch for extreme credibility of applicant in work setting	Someone to give a personal view of the applicant

Signature *Jack Allen*   **Date**   *12 October 1998*

How to resolve the tricky problem of the Personal Statement section of an application form (and not shoot yourself in the foot!)

Having seen a few application forms completed, it should be fairly obvious that the Personal Statement/Support Your Application section is the key to a winning application. This is scary in its own way, as a large white space waiting to be filled impressively without any helpful prompting. With other sections on the form there is a clearer 'knives go here, forks go there' cutlery tray feeling, but here applicants often experience a mind-numbing amnesia.

I have known many people complete application forms perfectly until they reach this section, where they fall apart. To be fair, most people can manage to write something down, but it is rarely totally relevant and even less likely to be interesting. Without wanting to make it more stressful, it has to be said that on this large white space battlefield, jobs are won or lost; your application will live or die by how you deal with this section, so only a positive, grab-it-by-the-throat attitude can work.

Remember, it does offer a freedom from the more structured sections to state your case, win friends and influence people. It can give a sort of catch-up space to applicants who start the race a little feebly; for example, less qualified or less experienced applicants can make up points by showing potential in this section.

This is also where transferable skills can be pulled out of the hat – those magic skills from one job that can be converted and found useful in a different job area. But you have to make the connection for the employer by detailing how, for example, your interpersonal skills gained from working on a charity committee could be turned to such good use in a commercial sales setting.

The amazing thing about this section is that, if you do it well, it may not even be necessary to provide proof of certain skills. If well planned, well written, and well organised, using persuasive and assumptive language, this section will itself provide evidence of important skills, such as:

- communication
- planning

- organisation
- self-marketing and
- sales

– and it is also a grandstand opportunity for showing self-confidence and motivation.

To gain a positive mind-set about the personal section, try being an employer for a moment. You have 30 applications to read in about an hour. What are you looking for? You probably want to know:

- What kind of person do I need?
- Who is this person really and do they match what I need?
- Why do they want the job?
- Can they do the job?
- What special skills or talents do they have to offer?
- How will they fit in?
- Can I see a spark of a real, breathing person behind the formal application form, or is it just a fake identity?
- Can this person make this company more successful?

As a prospective applicant you are probably interested in what an employer can do for you, but once having decided to apply, the applicant has to focus on what he or she can do for that employer in a very specific way, by finding out what that employer needs. Clearly, if as a result of a job advert analysis you can actually understand what an employer needs, it is a very small step to fulfil that need and in the process create a winning application.

So back to the terror of this large white space section with its lack of structure; to succeed and feel secure you need to impose a framework that supports and favours your application. This framework can be based on what little guidance the application offers in this section. An example of this might be:

> '*Please summarise why you feel you are suitable for this post. Reference should be made to previous experience, personal achievements and any other relevant information.*'

Start by analysing the details in the question and make short headings; in the above case they would be:

1. Why suitable for post
2. Previous experience
3. Personal achievements
4. Other relevant information

Then add in the employer's perspective to fill out these headings; then it would read like this:

1. Why suitable for post	*Why do they want the job?*
2. Previous experience	*Do they have what I need?*
	Can they do the job?
	What can they offer?
3. Personal Achievements	*What special talents?*
4. Other relevant information	*Who is this person really?*

What is created here is the structure for completing the 'Personal Statement' section effectively; what can make it interesting and lively is the choice of language (particularly power words, see page 40) and what I would call a positive or 'assumptive' turn of phrase.

Assumptive language

We all use assumptive language when we say things like 'See you soon', 'Bye for now', 'I look forward to seeing you', which doesn't necessarily mean much at all. However, there are two places in which assumptive language becomes meaningful, forceful and relevant: one in the 'large white space' section of an application form, the other in covering letters (see Chapter 10).

'Assumptive' can be understood as having a strong belief (often self-belief), being assured and confident, having a sense of conviction and credibility; so if your language is assumptive it displays all these impressive qualities. Better still, assumptive language uses phrases that are *presumptive* (in its most positive sense), because it implies: 'I am sure you will want to interview me.'

An hypnotic power is created by the use of strong and assertive 'I' phrases, like:

> *'I am a confident, positive person and I have experience of scientific technician work. I can work as part of a team but have experience of*

leading research projects. I also like to work on my own initiative and I can think creatively to come up with new solutions to problems.'

These 'I' phrases set up a sort of mesmerising rhythm, which nonetheless gives a sense of a real, living person behind the words. Assumptive language builds on this effect by using phrases that assume a positive outcome for the applicant; for example, the scientific technician above concluded her personal statement with:

'When I attend for interview, I will be glad to supply you with further proof of my suitability for this research post through examples of previous research awards. I look forward to meeting you.'

Note that this applicant writes 'When I attend' not 'If I attend for interview', with the implicit assumption that she will be shortlisted; this could be viewed as overweening arrogance, but is so lightly stated that it actually rings with self-belief; the final 'I look forward to meeting you' is polite and assured.

By reading some of the good application forms in this book it can be seen how effectively assumptive words and phrases can be used, most especially in the 'Personal Statement' section.

The 5-point plan for the great white space

1. Read the instructions/guidelines on the application form and note down the main points as skeleton headings (eg, previous experience, personal achievement to support your application).
2. From your job description psychoanalysis work out the employer's agenda and note down these points.
3. Work out a good reason for why you want the job (hopefully other than 'I just want to earn some money').
4. Work out the skills, abilities, or special talents you can offer and prove – ones that fit in with what the employer wants and needs (eg, your strange double jointedness might not be relevant to an insurance broker job, but might be highly appropriate for work in the circus).
5. Use a final assumptive sentence to conclude or close the sale!

Now it might help to look at a fairly standard, multipurpose Personal Statement framework to use as a guideline for your own.

Standard multipurpose Personal Statement framework

Why I want this job and what especially interests me about it
Example: *I am applying for the post of Nursery Nurse at St Bede's Children's Hospital, because I have substantial experience of working with children in various childcare contexts, in both educational and social care settings and am still enthralled and challenged by how children develop, learn and interact. I would particularly love to work with sick children to help them make up time lost from school through illness and/or to help stimulate them at a frustrating time. I understand something of the quality of care offered at St Bede's through my short-term volunteer placement last year.*

What I have to offer
Example: *I have worked with children of varying ages and abilities in one-to-one and small group situations, and can offer a caring attitude, patience, an interest in creative activities and music. I play the piano and guitar and have recently begun a course in sign language.*

Any personal achievements
Example: *A recent personal achievement for me was offering respite care to a child with severe behavioural difficulties, who needed 24-hour care, for a week, to enable her parents to have a break. Though hard work, I managed to survive the week and even felt I had built a relationship with the child.*

What the employer might want/need
Example: *I understand that this post requires someone who can cope with various ages of children with varying health problems and who can offer flexibility and breadth of experience, both of which I possess.*

Final assumptive concluding paragraph
Example: *I am a naturally cheerful, capable, adaptable person with good teamwork and interpersonal skills developed in my previous employment and I would enjoy the challenge of working in a hospital setting. I would be able to bring examples of creative and musical projects, undertaken with children, when I attend for interview.*

Obviously the headings used above are just memory joggers and would not be used on the final copy, but they do help to focus the mind when composing this section, and it is a good idea to arrange the section in paragraphs on the form to break the text up and make it more interesting and readable. Here is the final copy as it appeared on the application form.

Personal Section. Please summarise why you feel you are suitable for this post. Reference should be made to previous experience, personal achievements and any other relevant information

I am applying for the post of Nursery Nurse at St Bede's Children's Hospital, because I have substantial experience of working with children in various childcare contexts, in both educational and social care settings, and am still enthralled and challenged by how children develop, learn and interact. I would particularly love to work with sick children to help them make up time lost from school through illness and/or to help stimulate them at a frustrating time.

> Why the post interests applicant, and showing knowledge of the employer

I understand something of the quality of care offered at St Bede's through my short-term volunteer placement at the hospital last year.

> Experience offered

I have worked with children of varying ages and abilities in one-to-one and small group situations, and can offer a caring attitude, patience, an interest in creative activities and music. I play the piano and guitar and have recently begun a course in sign language.

> What employer wants/needs

A recent personal achievement for me was offering respite care to a child with severe behavioural difficulties, who needed 24-hour care, for a week, to enable her parents to have a break; though hard work, I managed to survive the week and I felt I had built a relationship with the child.

> Personal achievements

I understand that this post requires someone who can cope with various ages of children with varying health problems and who can offer flexibility and breadth of experience, both of which I possess.

I am a naturally cheerful, capable, adaptable person with good teamwork and interpersonal skills developed in my previous employment and I would enjoy the challenge of working in a hospital setting. I would be able to bring examples of creative and musical projects, undertaken with children, when I attend for interview.

> Assumptive conclusion with qualities and skills highlighted

By imposing a logical structure on this personal section, the style of writing actually seems natural and relevant, with a real sense of the human being behind the script; in addition, enthusiasm, through words like 'enthralled', and evidence of experience through voluntary experience and work history, are perfectly conveyed with a light touch.

A skeleton framework is displayed next to help you approach the 'Personal Statement' sections you meet in the future.

Skeleton framework for Personal Statement

Why I want this job and what especially interests me about it
What I have to offer
Any personal achievements
What the employer might want/need
Final assumptive concluding paragraph

Handwritten application forms

Most application forms fall into this category, and while content-wise the basic rules apply as mentioned earlier, surface impressions depend on well-presented layout and script. While few employers use graphology to analyse applications (Yes! Some do!), most are impressed by neat, readable handwriting and an orderly layout. So it is worth looking at some star examples of beautifully presented forms to fully appreciate the value of good surface impressions.

Example 1 Heather Tetlow

JOB APPLICATION FORM

Application for the post of:	ADMINISTRATIVE ASSISTANT
Surname:	TETLOW
Forename:	HEATHER
Address:	174 LOWER BANK ROAD HAMPTON HA4 6JL
First names:	HEATHER MARIE
Telephone No (Home):	01624 - 455 815
Date of Birth:	10.5.69

PREVIOUS EMPLOYMENT

Employer	From	To	Post details
HANLEYS BANK	1994	PRESENT	CUSTOMER SERVICE TELEPHONE ENQUIRIES
HAMPTON EVENING POST	1989	1984	TELESALES
PRINT MEDIA INC.	1987	1989	OFFICE JUNIOR

EDUCATION (Details of Secondary Schools and Colleges attended

School/College	From	To	Qualifications obtained
HAMPTON COLLEGE	1985	1987	BTEC BUSINESS ADMIN.
HAMPTON HIGH SCHOOL	1980	1985	5 O-LEVELS INCLUDING MATHS AND ENGLISH LANGUAGE

Details of any other relevant training, qualifications or experience

RSA LEVEL 3 WORD PROCESSING

CURRENTLY TAKING CITY AND GUILDS DESKTOP PUBLISHING

PERSONAL SECTION

Please complete this section, detailing interests and personal skills which might support your application

I am keen to work as an Administrative Assistant for the Youth Service because I have a wide experience of administrative work and a strong interest in young people, developed recently through voluntary youth work in Hampton.

My administrative experience has been in financial customer service areas, but I would like the chance to be part of a more caring service involving direct contact with the public. As the post also requires reception and telephone work, I believe my telephone skills used in telesales for the local newspaper will be very useful.

In addition, I have developed my information technology skills, most recently through RSA Level 3 at a local college, and I am currently studying for a desktop publishing diploma. This would enable me to help you with the advertising and promotion of the Youth Service at peak times.

I am organised, hard-working and patient, with good interpersonal skills. I believe these would be ideal qualities for the post of Administrative Assistant with the Youth Service.

Give the names and addresses of two referees below

JOHN SMITH 2 BALFOUR STREET HAMPTON HA4 7NT	MARY BROWN 66 ARKWRIGHT AVENUE OVER HAMPTON HA3 322

Signature   H. Tetlow

Date 18.12.97

Example 2 Jeannie Cameron

JOB APPLICATION FORM

Application for the post of: *LIBRARY ASSISTANT*

Surname: *CAMERON*

Forename: *JEANNIE*

Address: *8, SCOTS CRESCENT*
LANGTON,
CUMBRIA   CR8 FN4

First names: *JEAN MARIE*

Telephone No (Home): *0100 55776*

Date of Birth: *9 SEPTEMBER 1979*

PREVIOUS EMPLOYMENT

Employer	From	To	Post details
SWEETLEYS BOOKSHOP (SATURDAY WORK FOR 3 YEARS)	*1993*	*1996*	*Sales assistant, dealing with customers, taking orders and recently promoted to stock control*
University of Hampton (school work experience)	*November 1995*	*2 weeks only*	*Library assistant with academic librarians*

EDUCATION (Details of Secondary Schools and Colleges attended

School/College	From	To	Qualifications obtained
HAMPTON HIGH	*1991*	*1996*	*8 GCSES including Maths English Language, English Literature, History, French, Science, Information Technology* *B grades in all subjects*

Details of any other relevant training, qualifications or experience

Three years as school librarian with training in databases and CD Rom technology.

Responsibility for training other library assistants.

Please complete this section, detailing interests and personal skills which might support your application

I have always been interested in working in libraries, as I have enjoyed reading and spending time in both academic and public libraries, especially for my GCSE course work.

My school work experience at a university library gave me an insight into a different side of this type of work, and I had the chance to use high level academic databases to help students.

Having been trained as a school librarian, I was given the responsibility to train new library assistants, and it helped me understand the work of a library on a small scale; it also developed my training skills.

I am an organised, thorough, hardworking person and enjoy working in a team, and would like a career where I could offer a service to the public. I appreciate the value of a free public library service and would want to be part of one.

Give the names and addresses of two referees below

ANYONE (Personal) ANYWHERE (address)	ANYONE 2 (School/College or Employer) ANYWHERE 2
Signature J. Cameron.	Date 17/12/97

A worthwhile recap before trudging deeper into the application form jungle

APPLICATION FORM DON'TS

✗ Don't write final copy in pencil – most employers specify black pen and legible handwriting.

✗ Don't leave the form on the breakfast table and get porridge on it.

✗ Don't sneeze, spit or cough on it. Try to keep it in a plastic wallet to preserve appearance.

✗ Don't fold it up and carry it around in your pocket for a few days.

✗ Don't ignore the instructions – it makes employers very cross.

✗ Don't send it in late.

✗ Don't change handwriting styles in mid form.

✗ Don't tell lies on the form – make sure you keep a copy, so you can remember what you said!

CHAPTER *9*

Graduate and management level application forms...

...the same but different

If the simpler application forms can be compared to a cutlery tray (plastic), with slightly more complex ones being just a cutlery tray with personality (wooden), then graduate or management type forms can be viewed as, at best, just the same (mahogany) but with a more devious personality or, at worst, something with labyrinthine qualities and psychotic tendencies!

Of course, they reflect the mind of the application form writer, and the employer, just as all forms do. But they often have a higher if somewhat depressing goal, that is, to sift out not only the dross but anyone who does not fulfil the specific and exacting criteria devised by the recruiter. These criteria have often been developed through quite scientific, psychometric investigation of previously successful applicants; they are often based on a profile of a dream applicant, a kind of amalgamation of all that has been good, true and effective in past applicants, who have gone on to achieve great things in that organisation.

While the criteria might appear to be flawed, and occasionally overlook more individual applicants who do not exactly fit the profile, many employers are loath to turn away from a blueprint which has worked well in many cases. So the form with its more complex goals displays a mix of the familiar, the seemingly straightforward and the more complicated, often diabolical questions that frequently trap the unwary and almost terrify those who are easily alarmed.

In reality this type of form is still just a cutlery tray, but not the one that you know so well at at home. It is like one in someone else's house, with someone else's organisation and someone else's knives, forks, spoons, with steak knives and fish knives thrown in! It will take a little more time, but eventually you will realise (after some thought and practice) that it is just as familiar and easy to deal with as your own cutlery tray.

Basically the graduate or management type application form has more to accomplish from the employers' point of view but, by analysing it and the job requirements, it is an easy process to create a winning application. Remember to follow the step-by-step procedure suggested previously, most particularly:

- X-ray the advert
- dissect the job description and personnel specification
- decide key skills, abilities and personal qualities and
- match them to employers' requirements.

In addition, for higher level jobs, applicants are expected to show a greater knowledge of the company or organisation, not just from what can be surmised from employers' literature, but through what might be described as 'detective work', through company reports, informal contacts and financial publications. This is not simply essential for the interview stage of the recruitment procedure, but also for the application form, where there may be a chance to show this knowledge.

So let's look at one version of a graduate application form. It may appear abbreviated, but in its very brevity lurks its worst danger. Be sure that if the form offers minimal space to supply information, its purpose is to see how someone can summarise and condense facts in a succinct and meaningful way.

Graduate Application Form

Please complete this form in **black** ink or typescript with shaded section in **block capitals**

Reference number A56 For Office Use		Name of employer	
Present/most recent university		Vacancy/Post	
Surname	Basic information sections – ensure accuracy of details and read instructions	First names	
Home address		Term time address (if different)	
Date of birth		Country of birth	

Secondary/ Further Education School/College	From	To	Exams studied with qualifications gained
			Grades and subjects are important

University name	From	To	Type of degree/diploma Class expected/obtained
	Specify HND, ordinary or honours degree with main and subsidiary subjects		

Postgraduate qualifications

University	From	To	PhD/MA/Dip	Title of course or research
	Any sort of post-degree training should be detailed here, whatever its duration			

Any other qualifications or skills, eg keyboard, languages, computer literacy

Match any skills required by employer with those you possess. Don't forget unusual ones like language fluency, especially sign language, or First Aid.

Activities and Interests: Give details of your main interests

Try to mention relevant interests or activities which show commendable or desirable qualities. Use full sentences with 'I' statements. instructions

Work Experience
[Include sandwich placements, temporary, voluntary and vacation work]
Employer name   From   To   Type of work

> Many graduates have minimal work experience but need to
> detail the full range of vacation, temporary or short-term
> work to prove employability and to showcase skills and
> abilities, actual or potential, demanded by employers.

Choice of career: explain interest in choice of career and give evidence of suitability

> The clues here are in the instructions – 'Explain interest', that is why you
> want the job and what you have to offer, and 'give evidence', that is show
> proof that you can do it by mention of experience or academic ability.

Show how aspects of work experience or academic courses relate to career choice.

> Some people gain nothing from experience or academic
> study, so you have to show what has been developed in
> you, which could be of interest to the employer.

Any other relevant information in support of your application

> The 'Something Else' factor that shows you want
> the job and have what other applicants may lack!

References (one Academic, one Personal)

> Don't forget this bit
> or your signature!

Signature

It all looks fairly simple, but the preparation and analysis has to be done beforehand with, if anything, more rigour; otherwise applicants very quickly become entrapped. Remember that small sections may seem innocuous, but it is always harder to summarise in a few words without omitting vital facts. It is important, if handwriting the form, to do the practice copies in pencil with ruled paper behind the form for tidiness, and to work out the exact number of words that can be neatly squeezed into each section.

Handwritten examples follow: two for a Marketing Trainee, completed first in a fairly cursory fashion, then in a more winning way. The third is a good example of a self-aware, self-confident applicant who shows commitment and enthusiasm for her chosen career.

Ben Mark 1

This first form appears to have been done in a hurry, with reasonable information sections but curt subtext/subjective sections. It seems the applicant doesn't want or can't be bothered to reveal himself, which is a serious error. Above all there is no feeling of a real person – no enthusiasm and certainly no evidence to back up statements. Unfortunately this is typical of someone who has misread the form both at an objective level (no referees are given) and at a subjective level.

<table>
<tr><td colspan="5" align="center">GRADUATE APPLICATION FORM
Please complete this form in black ink or typescript
with shaded section in block capitals</td></tr>
<tr><td colspan="3">Reference number A56
For Office Use</td><td colspan="2">Name of employer
HOLY SPORTS</td></tr>
<tr><td colspan="3">Present/Most recent university
HAMPTON UNIVERSITY</td><td colspan="2">Vacancy/Post
MARKETING TRAINEE</td></tr>
<tr><td colspan="3">Surname   CAMERON</td><td colspan="2">First names   BEN</td></tr>
<tr><td colspan="3">Home address
8 BLOGGS LANE
HOTTINGHAM
SURREY</td><td colspan="2">Term time address (if different)
HAMPTON UNIVERSITY
HAMPTON
SURREY</td></tr>
<tr><td colspan="3">Date of birth   09|09|76</td><td colspan="2">Country of birth   U.K.</td></tr>
<tr><td>Education
School/College</td><td>From</td><td>To</td><td colspan="2">Exams studied with
qualifications gained</td></tr>
<tr><td>ALL SOULS HIGH</td><td>1987</td><td>1994</td><td colspan="2">GCSEs: English (C), English Lit (B), Maths (C) Home Ec (C), RE (C), Science (B/B) History (B), French (B)</td></tr>
<tr><td>University name
HAMPTON UNI</td><td>From
1994</td><td>To
1997</td><td colspan="2">Type of degree/diploma   BA
Class expected/obtained   2:1</td></tr>
<tr><td colspan="5">Postgraduate qualifications</td></tr>
<tr><td>University</td><td>From</td><td>To</td><td>PhD/MA/Dip</td><td>Title of course
or research</td></tr>
<tr><td colspan="5">Any other qualifications or skills, eg keyboard, languages, computer literacy
RSA C.L.A.I.T. Computer Literacy and Information Technology</td></tr>
</table>

Activities and Interests. Give details of your main interests

Football, Tennis & Films

Work Experience
[Include sandwich placements, temporary, voluntary and vacation work]

Employer name	From	To	Type of work
The Black Sheep	1992	1994	Glass collecting / barwork
Incentives Company Limited	July 1995	Sept 1995	Vacation work setting up business conferences

Choice of career: explain interest in choice of career and give evidence of suitability.

Working in the marketing of a sports manufacturer will suit me because I have a long-standing interest in sport

Show how aspects of work experience or academic courses relate to career choice.

The marketing modules on my course have given me an understanding of this subject.

Any other relevant information in support of your application

I'm an outgoing, commercially minded person and would be an assett to your company

References (one Academic, one Personal)

Signature   *Ben Cameron*   Date   27/12/97

Ben Mark 2

Appearance-wise, this is a better form, with more care taken over presentation and a fuller personal profile; detail about writing for a football magazine, vacation work and course projects is relevant and more convincing. Nonetheless, this form betrays the fact that the applicant is not fully self-aware of his own talents and not completely informed of the employer's needs, by analysis of the job description. It is a good enough application form but lacks conviction.

GRADUATE APPLICATION FORM
Please complete this form in **black** ink or typescript
with shaded section in **block capitals**

Reference number A56 For Office Use	Name of employer HOLY SPORTS
Present/Most recent university HAMPTON UNIVERSITY	Vacancy/Post MARKETING TRAINEE
Surname CAMERON	First names BEN
Home address 8 BLOGGS LANE HOTTINGHAM SURREY	Term time address (if different) HAMPTON UNIVERSITY HAMPTON SURREY
Date of birth 09 9 76	Country of birth U.K.

Education School/College	From	To	Exams studied with qualifications gained			
ALL SOULS HIGH	1987	1994	GCSEs: English C English Lit B Home Ec C History B	Maths C RE C Science B/B French B		
University name HAMPTON UNIVERSITY	From 1994	To 1997	Type of degree/diploma BA Class expected/obtained 2:1			

Postgraduate qualifications	NOT APPLICABLE			
University	From	To	PhD/MA/Dip	Title of course or research

Any other qualifications or skills, eg keyboard, languages, computer literacy

RSA C.L.A.I.T. (COMPUTER LITERACY AND INFORMATION TECHNOLOGY)

Activities and Interests. Give details of your main interests

I am a keen player and supporter of football.
I also write for a local football club's fan
magazine.

Work Experience
[Include sandwich placements, temporary, voluntary and vacation work]

Employer name	From	To	Type of work
The Black Sheep Public House	1992	1994	Glass collecting and barwork – NVQ in Hospitality and Catering achieved.
Incentives Company Limited	July 1945	Sept 1945	Vacation work involving setting up business conferences.

Choice of career: explain interest in choice of career and give evidence of suitability.

I have a long-standing interest in sport, and through my
vacation work as a conference organiser, I realised I
have a talent for dealing with business clients and could
use this in a sports marketing context.

Show how aspects of work experience or academic courses relate to career choice.

The marketing modules and work-based projects on my
course have given me and understanding of and
enthusiasm for marketing.

Any other relevant information in support of your application

I am outgoing, commercially minded and have strong
interpersonal skills, and I believe I could be an
asset to your company.

References (one Academic, one Personal)

Professor E Redknapp, Hampton University
Mr. R. Berry, Marketing Director, Hampton F.C

Signature	Ben Cameron	Date	27/12/97

Clare – a winning application

This form is well presented, has a natural style and is convincing in the motivation of the applicant. There is proof of skills gained through temporary work and a genuine interest in the choice of career.

GRADUATE APPLICATION FORM				
Please complete this form in **black** ink or typescript with shaded section in **block capitals**				
Reference number A56 For Office Use			Name of employer HALE AND HEARTY	
Present/Most recent university HAMPTON			Vacancy/Post RETAIL MANAGEMENT	
Surname SCOTT			First names CLARE	
Home address 5 SUSSEX GARDENS, CHERRINGTON, SUSSEX SN8 5ZH			Term time address (if different) HAMPTON UNIVERSITY HAMPTON, SURREY SRN 2PQ	
Date of birth 2.2.76			Country of birth UK	
Education School/College	From	To	Exams studied with qualifications gained	
St. Joseph's High	1987	1994	GCSEs in English (A) Maths (C) History (A) French (B) German (B) Biology (C) Art (C) A levels French (A) English (C) German (B)	
University name HAMPTON UNIVERSITY	From 1994	To 1997	Type of degree/diploma BUSINESS B.A. HONOURS Class expected/obtained 2:2	
Postgraduate qualifications				
University HAMPTON UNIVERSITY	From July 97	To Sept 97	PhD/MA/Dip Intensive French Dip.	Title of course or research French
Any other qualifications or skills, eg keyboard, languages, computer literacy				
A recent diploma course in spoken French has refreshed my conversational French. I am confident with many commercial computer packages.				

Activities and Interests. Give details of your main interests

I am interested in health and fitness, in particular healthy eating. I play netball for the university team. I love going to the cinema with friends.

Work Experience
[Include sandwich placements, temporary, voluntary and vacation work]

Employer name	From	To	Type of work
Beatleys Supermarket	1992	1994	Saturday work and summer placements gave me experience of retailing.
Superfit Health Studios	1994	1997	Part time work as a fitness adviser on fitness and dietary programmes with various clients.

Choice of career: explain interest in choice of career and give evidence of suitability.

I want to work for a wholefood retailer to share my experience of a healthy lifestyle through diet and nutrition. I have a sound retail background and my business degree has developed by business acumen. I am good with people and find that I lead by example.

Show how aspects of work experience or academic courses relate to career choice.

As a project module on my degree course, I worked at an organic food farm, creating an advertising strategy, which was used subsequently in a successful advertising campaign for their products.

Any other relevant information in support of your application

I am outgoing, confident and hardworking with good communication and team work skills. In my retail experience I have had considerable customer service experience.

References (one Academic, one Personal)

Mr M. Smith
Beatleys Supermarket
Hampton, Surrey S10 5PN

Professor D. Suleman
Hampton University
Hampton, Surrey
SRN 2PQ

Signature Clare Scott   Date 10 February '98

Now a wordprocessed version, just to emphasise how much can be conveyed in this fairly restricted format. If you are still left feeling that it has not been possible to paint the full picture of you, it may be allowable to submit a CV with the form, as long as this has not been expressly precluded in the application package.

GRADUATE APPLICATION FORM
Please complete this form in **black** ink or typescript
with shaded section in **block capitals**

Reference number A56 **For Office Use**	Name of employer HAVERSHAM ESTATES
Present/Most recent university HAMPTON UNIVERSITY	Vacancy/Post ASSISTANT SURVEYOR
Surname WYATT	First names PHILIP
Home address 12 GLENBUCK DRIVE HAMPTON, SURREY GO6 5YT	Term time address (if different)
Date of birth 6 JANUARY 1974	Country of birth UK

Education School/College	From	To	Exams studied with qualifications gained
Hampton High	1985	1990	GCSEs: English (B); Maths (A); Physics with Chemistry (B); Biology (C); Geography (B); History (C); German (C); Statistics (A); French (C)
Hampton College	1990	1992	A levels: Economics (A); History (B); English (C)

University name Hampton University	From 1992	To 1995	Type of degree/diploma BSc Estate Management (Honours) Class expected/obtained 2:2 obtained

Postgraduate qualifications		Not Applicable	
University	From	To	PhD/MA/Dip Title of course or research

Any other qualifications or skills, eg keyboard, languages, computer literacy

From my recent volunteer work with the RSPB I have gained computer skills and have achieved a basic competency in path laying, fence and hide building and tree planting. I have also had the chance to work with various environmental professionals, which has further developed my interpersonal and teamwork skills.

Activities and Interests. Give details of your main interests

I have always enjoyed outdoor activities, including walking, canoeing and fishing and have a keen interest in environmental issues. I have particularly liked being involved with conservation projects to restore country areas using traditional crafts; through these interests I have been lucky enough to be trained in the basic practical craft skills, which as a conservation volunteer I have had to use whatever the weather!

Work Experience
[Include sandwich placements, temporary, voluntary and vacation work]

Employer name	From	To	Type of work
Henley Agricultural Supplies	November 1989	2 weeks only	School work experience dealing with local farmers in farm shop
Hampton Estate	Summer 1990/1991/1992	5 weeks	Handyman assistant on estate helping with deer and birds in the mornings with average 5am start; afternoon responsibility for visitor activities with estate supervisor.
Bellystone Natural Park, USA	Summer 1993, then 1995–1996	8 weeks, then 1 year contract on graduation	Park assistant, involved in park maintenance and conservation and visitor attractions. Particular responsibility for bears and picnic areas, with all the problems and challenges these created.

Choice of career: explain interest in choice of career and give evidence of suitability.

I want to work as an estates manager because of my interest in the countryside and conservation and because this type of work will use my experience of environmental work through vacation and gap year employment and my strong practical/outdoor skills. I know I am suitable for this kind of work because I like the variety it offers and the way it utilises my strengths and abilities, and I can offer an employer commitment and enthusiasm.

Show how aspects of work experience or academic courses relate to career choice.

Both work experience and academic study have developed my surveying and environmental skills; in particular, a project for restoring a woodland area, undertaken while a student, resulted in a local award. Working in America helped me develop further experience by looking at other ways of dealing with the conservation of an area of outstanding natural beauty, and fired me with enthusiasm for the management of the countryside in ways to benefit everyone.

Any other relevant information in support of your application

Business modules on my recent course of study have made me understand the financial considerations of the management of country estates in a realistic light. Conservation volunteer work over a number of years has given me flexibility and the ability to work in a team.

References (one Academic, one Personal)

Prof G Stringer	Ms T Brewer
Surveying Dept, Hampton University	Hampton Estates
Hampton HA42 3PA	Hampton HA42 6JH

Signature P Wyatt   Date 2nd February 1998

As can be clearly seen, Philip Wyatt's application form is quite packed, and it has a pervasive theme:

'I am interested and talented in surveying and environmental skills and have motivation and determination to do well in this career, so be persuaded to interview me!'

Note how every available space is completely filled, making full use of the opportunity to sell himself, but neatly presented so the text is legible. Also the words are used very effectively to give a clear idea of personality with the occasional humorous touch (such as bears and picnic areas – how could anyone read that without thinking of Yogi Bear?), and someone in the middle of sifting through large numbers of forms might welcome this light relief! It is worth noting the use of words and phrases which invigorate Philip's application:

'flexibility'
'fired with enthusiasm'
'5am start'
'challenges and problems'
'practical and outdoor skills'
'in all weathers'.

These aspects of the job were all suggested by the subtext of the job advert and were impressively conveyed on the application form.

If concise forms have their pitfalls, then longer forms come with their own set of dangers. Some graduate employers choose to use a standard application form (SAF), designed by the Association of Graduate Recruiters. It is basically an extended version of the graduate form just shown with larger sections and more space for information, and a few extra questions about the benefits of any work experience and preference for geographical locations.

This form is available at university careers services nationwide, which can offer professional graduate careers guidance as well. In essence, if the sections are dealt with in a planned and considered way, they should be no problem, but remember the painstaking approach suggested earlier in this book as a foolproof way of preparation.

Employers' own unstandardised application forms for graduate and or management type jobs are less easy to quantify, as they may have standard information only sections mixed in with rather unusual or challenging questions. These quirky questions place greater demands on intellectual agility and transferable skills, which, of course, they are designed to test. They are not as free spirited as the 'Personal Statement' section, as they are both specific, objective and subjective in tone. The only way to tame them is to analyse them, as suggested for job adverts and application information, and X-ray them down at least to their underwear. Once seen in this light they will lose any power to alarm.

Quirky questions and how to deal with them

Let's look at some free expression ones first, where you have to create the structure or format.

1. Describe an event where your organisational skills achieved a successful outcome.

They are assuming you have organisational skills and you have to think of an occasion when they worked to your advantage. Examples might be a vacation work experience, some charitable work, a team work situation. Make sure you give proof of the success of the event and remember that a lightweight event, like successfully running a children's party (entertainments organised and fractious tempers soothed) can be just as impressive as something rather serious.

2. Describe an occasion when you led a group. How did you motivate the group to achieve the desired result?

This is, of course, the motivational, teamwork, leadership question and it needs to be shown that you involved the group in deciding what needed to be accomplished and that challenges and problems were discussed and anticipated; roles within the group should then have been assigned, with a clear action plan being approved by all team members and everyone aware of time deadlines and targeted outcomes. Think of a course project or school college committee work for ideas for this.

3. Describe a problem that you encountered. Show how you dealt with it and produced a solution.

This is the 'show your problem-solving/analytical skills' question. Think of all the problems you have encountered, from how to survive on a grant, how to get a well-paid vacation job, to how to entertain three bored youngsters on a wet Bank Holiday. You are bound to have been successful in some way, so show the thought process, the research you undertook (finding out cheap deals; discovering which employers offered the best student packages; rooting out free activities locally...) and the way you made your decision, weighing up all the options, and then detail the solution.

4. Think of a conflict you dealt with and say how you handled it

Most people, while agreeing that their lives are full of conflict, struggle to summon up a suitable circumstance for this one; but again look for the simple day-to-day conflicts like flat sharers arguing about who cleans the kitchen or persuading an inebriated friend to take a taxi home rather than drive. The stuff of ordinary life is full of conflict and tricky situations you may have handled well.

5. Tell us what attracted you to BLANK plc

They want you to be specific and show knowledge of the company, which is why it is so vital that you research the organisation before applying. Mention public perception of the company (do a quick ballot among your friends!) and some current financial issue; finish with your own view of the company and why that company ethos suits you. Try and be complimentary without being fawning!

6. What do you believe are your key skills? When and how have you best demonstrated these?

If you have done a realistic self-assessment you will find these questions easy (see Back-of-a-postage-stamp self-analysis, page 42); look for evidence in work experience and academic situations. Explain how well your communication skills were used, for example, as editor of a school poetry magazine where you both wrote and selected poems for publication, and dealt with the hurt feelings of rejected poets as well!

Some companies use similar questions but actually give advice or a format for answering them, but in fact the types of these questions fall into six neat categories, which pan out something like this:

- state your key skills
- show your organisational/planning skills
- prove your leadership/teamwork skills (particularly for management type jobs)
- explain how you solved a problem
- describe a conflict or challenge overcome.

It is clear that the questions are devised to seek out those skills that employers value and that make applicants highly employable, so if you feel any of the above skills are underdeveloped, it may be wise to look for ways of improving them.

A useful format for breaking down these questions is given in the following sample questions. It shows how much more manageable they can become if you use your X-ray eyes.

Example 1
Using a specific example, show how as a group leader you directed the group to achieve a desired result.

The situation:

The action you took:

The outcome:

Example 1
Give an example of how you tackled a complex problem, the research you undertook and the steps you took to solve it.

The situation:

The action you took:

The outcome:

So a fail-safe format for dealing with these types of questions is invariably the 'quirky questions mantra', which goes like this:

> Situation
> Action
> Outcome.

Follow these headings and you are bound to answer in a logical, comprehensive way.

To finish, it is worth looking at some typical formula answers to quirky questions, just to clarify how easy it is — they are only examples and meant to stimulate you to come up with ideas of your own!

One way of dealing with question type three...

Describe a problem that you encountered. Show how you dealt with it and produced a solution.

As a 17-year-old babysitter, I was left in sole charge of two young children, one on medication. The parents were used to me and placed great confidence in me, often returning at 2 or 3 in the morning; I normally stayed the night, but was aware of them returning. On one occasion they had not returned at 4am and I began to be concerned.   (The Situation)

I considered all the possible reasons for their lateness but decided to refrain from taking action till the early morning; I decided that they were often late and might have decided to drive back in the early morning. The youngest child's medication was due at 8am, so I determined to wake at 6am, and reassess the situation. I had been left no phone number or details of the parents' whereabouts.   (The Action)

At 5am the parents returned with apologies for their lateness — they had lost track of the time through an engrossing game of bridge! I was glad I had not panicked, but asked to be left accurate contact information for future occasions.
                                    (The Outcome)

This may appear rather a humdrum problem, with inaction rather than action being highlighted, but in fact the ability to cope and not panic, the ability to make a considered decision at quite a young age, when over-reaction and a phone call to Mum might have been more usual, is very commendable. This answer conveys the impression of an articulate, rational, responsible and capable applicant.

An approach to question type four…

Think of a conflict you dealt with and say how you handled it.

In a summer vacation job as a library assistant, the most common cause of conflict was the payment of fines for overdue books. On one occasion, a lady was highly irate to be asked to pay a fine for a book she assured me she had returned. She had received a (rather abrupt) standard notification of fines letter at a time of bereavement and ill health and came into the library at a busy time prepared to cause a very nasty scene. (The Situation)

I realised that to argue with this lady without checking all the facts would fuel her anger, and with a queue forming felt under pressure to react, but knew that the library insisted on fines being paid. So I called for help from a colleague to deal with the queue and then took the lady to one side and asked her if she could help me gain a full picture of the situation so I could deal with this problem. (The Action)

After some assurances on my part that I was not trying to fob her off, she gave me the full details; I explained the library procedure for tracing a lost book, apologised for the fact that she had had to deal with this problem at a time of bereavement and promised to look for the book personally that day. I was able to put a temporary stop on the fine and confirmed that if in fact it was our mistake she would get a full apology. At this point she began to cry with pent-up emotion and relief that I had been kind, and five minutes and a glass of water later, she was able to leave the library. Later in the day I phoned her to say the book had been found, the fine had been cancelled and a letter of apology was in the post. (The Outcome)

Again a rather common situation is described, but with a fair amount of stress and embarrassment attached; this applicant shows calmness under pressure, good customer service and kindness – all very commendable qualities.

So finally remember that on these kinds of application forms a picture of you on top form is meant to shine out, and with planning and preparation it will be possible to do this with confidence and enthusiasm.

For any kind of application form the three magic 'E's are vital:
Enthusiasm
Evidence of skills and experience
Employability (how useful you will be to that employer).

If on a final scan of a completed application form these three 'E's are manifest, you will know you have created a winning application.

CHAPTER 10 Covering letters – the valued friend

Think of a covering letter as that devoted friend who ushers you into parties and introduces you to everyone, always mentioning your best qualities, ensuring a warm welcome. This letter takes the application form or CV by the hand and, complementing and complimenting it, ensures a fair hearing, or rather reading. In some cases, where application forms or CVs are considered identical on merit, the covering letters are judged as a back-up to assess any other apparent talents. So let's look at the vital statistics of a covering letter:

- it can accompany a CV or application form as a matter of courtesy
- it can reinforce key points from the accompanying form or CV (without being unduly repetitive)
- it needs to be brief and to the point (no more than three paragraphs)
- it needs a good, unwaffly beginning
- it should say what you want to do for that employer
- it should say how you are suited to the work
- it should finish with an assumptive sentence (a good ending).

Obviously the style of the covering letter should match the CV or application form and the nature of the employment applied for; the letter should be in a reasonably formal business letter format but, depending on the type of job, a more formal or informal style might be more appropriate. For example, for the legal profession, an articulate, professional, formal letter would be required, whereas for the media or advertising a more pushy, lively style would be expected.

Resist the impulse to rush off a letter that says something like *'Here's my CV – I hope you like it!'* The basic format should follow the guidelines below, but be confident enough to individualise it.

Basic Covering Letter Format

Your address including
postcode and telephone number
on the right

Name and abbreviated
address of company on left

Date of letter
under your address

Dear Sir/Madam or name of employer (Mr Wright/Ms Ford)

Re: (Title of job as advertised)

First paragraph, first sentence: What you are applying for and why. If possible show knowledge of employer. Second sentence: Refer to CV or application form and draw attention to one or two specific details.

Second paragraph, first sentence: Why you are especially suited to the job and what you can do for the employer (based on analysis of job description). Second sentence: Any relevant experience you can cite.

Third paragraph: Availability for interview and assumptive sentence.

Yours faithfully (if Dear Sir/Madam) or Yours sincerely (if named person)

A typical business letter format would then look something like the one on the next page.

Your address including
postcode telephone number
on the right

Name and abbreviated
address of company on left

Date of letter
under your address

Dear Ms Ford

Re: (Title of job as advertised) *Legal Executive*

First paragraph, first sentence: What you are applying for and why. If possible show knowledge of employer.

I am applying for the above post because I have recently completed a law degree and want to be able to use my legal and research skills in a law clinic context. I am familiar with the Hampton Law Clinic through personal experience as a student dealing with a dispute with my flat landlord, and was impressed with the professionalism and helpfulness of the staff at that time.

Second sentence: Refer to CV or application form and draw attention to one or two specific details.

As will be seen from my attached CV I have been involved with a law department project offering advocacy for homeless people and believe I have good experience of dealing with a variety of clients in fairly difficult circumstances.

Second paragraph, first sentence: Why you are especially suited to the job and what you can do for the employer (based on analysis of job description)
Second sentence – any relevant experience you can cite.

I believe that contacts made in the local housing department through the advocacy project and my legal training have developed the communication and listening skills and research ability needed for this job. In addition I am keen to be part of a community law clinic, which has such a clear purpose and valued role.

Third paragraph: Availability for interview and assumptive sentence.

I am available for interview at your convenience and I look forward to meeting you.

Yours sincerely
Finish with 'Yours sincerely' if you have addressed the letter to a named person, 'Yours faithfully' if 'Dear Sir/Madam'.

See the final copy below. Your letter can be handwritten or typed depending on your preference and confidence in the legibility and neatness of your handwriting!

A good covering letter

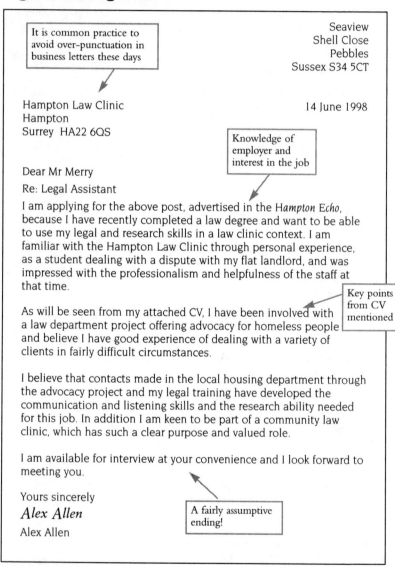

It is common practice to avoid over-punctuation in business letters these days

Seaview
Shell Close
Pebbles
Sussex S34 5CT

Hampton Law Clinic
Hampton
Surrey HA22 6QS

14 June 1998

Knowledge of employer and interest in the job

Dear Mr Merry

Re: Legal Assistant

I am applying for the above post, advertised in the *Hampton Echo*, because I have recently completed a law degree and want to be able to use my legal and research skills in a law clinic context. I am familiar with the Hampton Law Clinic through personal experience, as a student dealing with a dispute with my flat landlord, and was impressed with the professionalism and helpfulness of the staff at that time.

Key points from CV mentioned

As will be seen from my attached CV, I have been involved with a law department project offering advocacy for homeless people and believe I have good experience of dealing with a variety of clients in fairly difficult circumstances.

I believe that contacts made in the local housing department through the advocacy project and my legal training have developed the communication and listening skills and the research ability needed for this job. In addition I am keen to be part of a community law clinic, which has such a clear purpose and valued role.

I am available for interview at your convenience and I look forward to meeting you.

Yours sincerely
Alex Allen
Alex Allen

A fairly assumptive ending!

It is worth looking at another couple of sample of letters to understand the value of matching the type of letter to the type of employer and to appreciate the difference between a mildly assumptive ending and one that is a little stronger. The following letter was used by a graphic design student looking for a work placement in the highly competitive area of advertising design.

An alternative covering letter

7 St Mary's Road
Durber
Kent TN5 S4D

30th May 1998

Max Hatfield
Paragon Design Ltd
Bickhampton
Kent TN4 0HU

Dear Max Hatfield

A colleague of yours at Marriot Printing suggested I contact you with regard to a future work placement I need for eight weeks in the summer. I know your company specialises in photographic design work for advertising companies, which happens to be my speciality. On the second year of my course a design brief commissioned by Trumpett Advertising was assigned to me after my competitive bid was successful, and it has since been used in a major advertising campaign.

As can be seen from my CV, I have already had some experience of advertising through my college work experience and I am creative, enthusiastic and full of ideas. I would be glad to help with any type of design projects but would also like to experience the more commercial aspects of a design studio, doing basic office work, answering the telephone or making the tea.

I will be coming to London with my portfolio the week of 11–15 May. Is it possible to have an interview sometime during that week? I will telephone you in a couple of days to have your thoughts on the matter.

Thank you for your time.

Yours sincerely

Ella Maxwell

What you will notice about this letter is how natural and informal it sounds, while still maintaining a formal letter format. Using a named contact from another company is the kind of name dropping that is called 'networking' for serious job seekers. Notice also how key points from the CV are mentioned, with good self-awareness of personal qualities and the flexibility to be prepared to do anything from design work to making the tea!

Finally, as assumptive endings go, this is the best – both polite and confident that the employer will want to speak to her. Following up a speculative letter or CV is always a good idea anyway.

A further sample letter follows, again to convey how different these letters can sound while retaining the same basic format.

Another version of a covering letter

Mereside
Mere Close
Bromton
BR6 7TH

Mr R Spencer   1 March 1998
Headteacher
Bromton High
Bromton BR12 6FF

Dear Mr Spencer

Re: German/French Teacher

I enclose my CV in support of my application for the post of teacher of German/French as advertised in *Education Today*.

You will see from my details that I am in the middle of a post-graduate teaching course and am at present on teaching practice in Bromton Secondary School. I am a late entrant to the profession and will be 34 when I qualify in the summer, which I hope you will agree is an advantage in that I have a certain amount of life experience to bring to the classroom.

I shall be pleased to supply further details or attend for interview as required.

Yours sincerely

Marion Carr

That is a very concise covering letter which makes one rather brilliant point – slight maturity for a newly qualified teacher post. Assumptive language is used with a light touch when the applicant uses the phrase *'I hope you will agree'*. It is a good model for any covering letter.

Other good assumptive phrases that can be used at the appropriate point in letters are the following:

- *'I will phone next week to hear your views'* (after sending a speculative CV)
- *'I will phone next week to see if it is possible to meet you for an informal chat'* (when trying to stimulate interest in you as a potential employee)
- *'I would appreciate the chance to meet you and can attend for interview at your convenience'*
- *'I am happy to offer a short work trial as evidence of my skills'* (a good way to impress an employer).

Now you know everything there is to know about CVs, covering letters and applications. If you really give yourself the chance, and prepare and plan fully, there is every reason for your application form or CV or covering letter to stand out from the crowd and be a winner. And every time you are tempted to panic, calm yourself with mental pictures of jelly moulds and cutlery trays; always remember – if a job is worth applying for, it is worth applying for properly. Now you possess all the tools and know-how, go out and get the job of your dreams!